Spiritual Rivers

Jeanne Marie Guyon

REJUVENATED BOOKS

Series One

Spiritual Rivers
Rejuvenated Books: Series One
ISBN: 978-1-63171-003-2

Copyright ©2018 by Unorthodox Press. All rights reserved. Although the original text and many elderly English translations are now in the public domain, this rejuvenated paraphrase is a new creative work and fully protected by copyright law.

About this text: Jeanne-Marie Bouvier de la Motte Guyon, commonly referred to as Madame Guyon, was a wealthy French widow who practiced and promoted a form of Christian mysticism that became known as Quietism. This is her first published work, which was first published in 1682 and which has remained in print ever since. This paraphrase is based on:

> Guyon, Jeanne Marie Bouvier de la Motte Guyon. *Spiritual Torrents*. Translated by A. W. Marston. London: H. R. Allenson, Limited, 1875.

This book is printed in the United States of America.

Contents

- One: Three Ways of Seeking God 1
- Two: The First River 5
- Three: The Second River 15
- Four: The Third River — First Stage 23
- Five: Problems of the First Stage 37
- Six: The Third River — Second Stage 53
- Seven: The Third River — Third Stage 65
  1. The Plundering of the Soul 65
  2. The Second Stage
     of the Plundering of the Soul 78
  3. The Third Stage
     of the Plundering of the Soul 82
  4. The Soul's Entrance into Mystic Death . . . 92
- Eight: Consummation of the Third Stage . . 97
- Nine: The Third River — Fourth Stage . . . 105
- Ten: The Resurrection Life 123
- Eleven: The Abandoned Soul 129
- Twelve: Deformity 139
- Thirteen: Union with God 147

Poor souls who seek happiness in this life, you will never find it apart from God. Seek instead to return to God. In him, all your longings and troubles, your uneasiness and anxiety, will be reduced to perfect rest.

One

Three Ways of Seeking God

As soon as God brings his influence over a soul and the soul's return to him is true and sincere, there is first a cleansing of the soul through confession and repentance. Then God gives the soul a confident instinct to return to him completely and become united to him. The soul senses that it was not created for the amusements and trifles of the world. It has a center and a purpose to aim for, and apart from that purpose, it will never find true peace. This instinct is deeply embedded in the soul. It is more so in some and less so in others, but all have a loving urgency to purify themselves, to adopt the necessary ways and means of returning to their source and origin.

Spiritual Rivers

These souls are like rivers that, after leaving their source, flow continuously onward in order to bring themselves to the sea. Some rivers move seriously and slowly. Other rivers flow with greater speed. And some raging rivers rush to the sea with such frightful force that nothing can stop them. All the burdens that might be placed on them and all obstructions that might be set in their way to slow their course only serve to increase their violent journey to God.

The first type of souls move quietly towards holiness, never reaching the sea or only reaching it late in life. They are content to lose themselves in some stronger and more rapid river that carries them with itself into the sea.

Other souls—the second type of river—flow on more vigorously and promptly than the first. They even carry with them a number of smaller streams. These are more agreeable and useful. Their seriousness is pleasing. They're all loaded with shipping, and we sail upon them without fear or danger. However, these souls

Three Ways of Seeking God

are slow and idle in comparison with the third type.

The third type of souls rush onward with so much turbulence that they are utterly useless. They can't be navigated. No shipping can be trusted to them except in certain places and at certain times. These are bold, mad rivers that smash against the rocks, that terrify with their noise, and that stop at nothing.

With God's help, we will look at these three types of people, using the illustration of rivers that I have presented. We will begin with the first and conclude happily with the last.

Two

The First River

The first type of souls are those who, after their conversion, dedicate themselves to contemplation or even to works of charity. They perform some outward acts of self-denial. Little by little, they try to purify themselves, to rid themselves of certain obvious sins, and even of voluntary minor sins. They endeavor, with all their little strength, to advance gradually. However, their progress is feeble and slow.

Because the source of their flow is lacking, dryness sometimes causes delay. There are even periods, in times of drought, when they dry up altogether. They do not cease to flow from the source, but the flow is so weak that it's barely

Spiritual Rivers

perceptible. These rivers carry little or no freight to others, so to serve the public, it must be taken to them. Art must also assist nature and find ways to enlarge them with canals or with the help of other similar rivers that can be joined together. Once united, these rivers increase the amount of water flowing and, by helping each other, make themselves able to carry a few small boats — not to the sea but to some of the main rivers that we will speak of later.

People like this usually have little depth in their spiritual life. They work outwardly and rarely leave their meditations, so they are not fit for great things. In general, they carry no freight — that is to say, they can give nothing to others. God seldom uses them, unless it is to carry a few tiny boats — that is, to minister to physical needs. To be used at all, they must be poured into the canals of outward graces or united with others in religion. In this way, several streams of moderate grace manage to carry small boats. However, they do not reach the sea itself,

The First River

which is God. They never reach him in this life but only in the next.

Souls can still be purified in this way. There are many who pass for being very virtuous who never get beyond it. God gives them insights appropriate to their condition, and they are sometimes very beautiful, the admiration of the religious world. The most highly favored of this type are rigorous in their works of virtue. They invent thousands of holy methods and practices that will lead them to God and allow them to abide in his presence. However, it is all accomplished through their own human efforts, aided and supported by grace, so that their works seem to exceed the work of God, with his work only cooperating with theirs.

The spiritual life of this group only thrives in proportion to their outward work. If this work is removed, the progress of grace within them is stopped. They are like pumps, which only yield water in proportion to how actively they are operated. You see in them a great tendency to

Spiritual Rivers

support themselves with the help of their own natural feelings. You also see vigorous activity, a desire to be always doing something more and something new to promote their development. In seasons of barrenness, you see anxiety to free themselves of it.

They're subject to great fluctuations. Sometimes they work wonders, and at other times, they languish and decline. They have no steadiness in their work. Because the greater part of their religion is founded on natural feelings, whenever it happens that their resources run dry—either from lack of work on their part or lack of corresponding work on God's part—they fall into discouragement or double their efforts in the hope of finding in themselves the feelings they've lost. They never possess a deep peace or calmness in the midst of distractions. On the contrary, they're always on the alert to struggle against those distractions or to complain about them.

Souls like these should never be counseled to attempt passive devotion. It would ruin

The First River

them irrecoverably, taking from them their only means of seeking God. If people are forced to travel and have neither boat nor carriage nor any other alternatives than going by foot, and if you then remove their feet, you put travel beyond their reach. So it is with these souls. If you take away their works, which are their feet, they can never move forward. I believe this is the cause of the conflicts that trouble the religious world. Those who travel on the passive path, conscious of the blessedness they experience there, want to force everyone to travel with them. On the other hand, these who are in this first condition that I have described would like to confine everyone to their path, which would bring inestimable loss.

What then should be done? We must take the middle path and see for which of these two paths a soul is best suited. For some, this can be revealed by the opposition they have to remaining at rest and allowing the Spirit of God to lead them. It can by seen by the confusion of errors and weaknesses into which they fall

Spiritual Rivers

without being aware of them—or, if they are naturally prudent, by their skill in hiding their weaknesses from others and from themselves. The way to rescue them from such a condition is to guide them to live less in their minds and more in their hearts. If it appears that they are gradually substituting the heart for the mind, it's a sign that a spiritual work is being carried on within them.

I am at a loss to understand why such a loud complaint is raised against books that examine the inner life. I say that they can do no harm—except perhaps to those who are willing to lose themselves for the sake of their own pleasure, and for them, like spiders who convert flowers into venom, not only these things but everything else is harmful. However, to the humble souls who desire holiness, these books can do no harm because it is impossible for anyone to understand these things unless special insight has been given to them. Whatever others may read, they cannot correctly understand these

The First River

conditions that are beyond the scope of imagination and can only be understood through experience. The process of becoming holy moves forward steadily in accordance with the progress of the inner life. There are some who have advanced toward holiness and have faults that appear greater than those of others, but those faults are not the same in nature or degree.

The second reason why I say that these books can do no harm is that they demand so much death to human nature, so much breaking away, so many things to be conquered and destroyed. No one would ever have enough strength to do this without a sincere motive. Even if they were to try, it would only result in contemplation, which is to endeavor to destroy the self.

As for those who want to lead others down their own path and not down God's path, who wish to put barriers up against further advancement, who only know one way and want all the world do walk on it—as for them, I say that the evils that they bring upon others cannot

Spiritual Rivers

be remedied because they make others stop at certain points for the rest of their lives, and that prevents God from blessing them infinitely.

It seems to me that the life of holiness is like a school. The students are not kept in the same class. They're moved forward to other classes that are more advanced. Human knowledge, you are worth so little, yet people never fail to take every precaution with you. Knowledge of mystery and God, you are so great and so necessary, yet people neglect you, limit you, reduce you, and harm you. Oh, may there never be a school of religion. By wanting to make the knowledge of God a subject of study, people have marred it. They have tried to make rules and set boundaries for the Spirit of God, who has no boundaries.

Poor, powerless souls! You are better suited to God's purposes, and if you are faithful, your devotion will be more pleasing to him than that of the devotion of great minds who make prayer a subject of study rather than a practice. These poor souls who appear so powerless and so

The First River

incapable, however, are worthy of consideration. They must only knock at the door and wait with a humble patience until it opens to them.

The others of great intellect and sophisticated understanding cannot remain in silence before God for even a moment but make a continual Babel before him. They're able to give an account of their devotion in all its parts, and they always go through it according to their own will and with the same methods. They devote themselves as they wish on any subject that suggests itself to them. They're satisfied with themselves and with their understanding. They discuss at length the preparation and methods for prayer, but they make little progress in actual prayer. After ten or twenty years of this work, they remain the same.

When it's a question of loving a miserable creature, do they have a method for it? In that situation, the most unlearned are the most skillful. It is the same, and yet also very different, with loving God. Therefore, if people who have never understood this kind of religion come to

Spiritual Rivers

you to learn it, teach them to love God, to let themselves go with perfect abandonment into love, and they will soon understand it. If they have a nature that is slow to love, then let them do the best they can and wait patiently until love itself makes itself beloved in its own way, and not in yours.

Three

The Second River

The second type of souls is like those large rivers that move with a slow and steady flow. They flow with dignity and majesty. Their course is direct and easy to follow. They're given much freight and can flow to the sea without mingling with other rivers. However, because they are serious and slow, they take a long time to reach the sea. There are some that never reach it at all, losing themselves in other larger rivers or else turning aside to some arm of the sea. Many carry freight and are heavily loaded with it. They may be held back by floodgates and turned away at certain points.

These are the souls who travel in the passive way of seeing. Their strength is abundant. They

Spiritual Rivers

are laden with gifts, graces, and heavenly favors. They're the admiration of their generation. Many saints who shine as the stars in the church have never surpassed these boundaries. This class of souls is composed of two types. The first begins in the ordinary way and afterwards is drawn to passive contemplation. The others are taken by surprise, as it were. They are seized by the heart, and they feel themselves loving without having learned to know the object of their love.

There is this difference between divine and human love—human love requires a previous acquaintance with its object. Because it exists outside oneself, one's senses must take it in, and the senses can only take it in when the object is before them. The eyes see, and then the heart loves. Divine love isn't like this. God has absolute power over the human heart, and because he is its source and its end, it isn't necessary for him to first reveal himself to it. He takes the heart by force without giving it battle. The heart is powerless to resist him. He doesn't need to use

The Second River

absolute and violent authority—unless it is in some cases where he permits that—in order to manifest his power. Instead, he takes hearts by making them burn in a moment, and usually he gives them flashes of light that dazzle them, lifting them closer to himself.

To those without divine discernment, these souls appear to be greater than those of whom I will speak later. Outwardly, they achieve a high degree of holiness because God noticeably expands their natural capacity and replenishes it in an extraordinary way. However, they're never really brought to a state of dying to self. God doesn't usually draw them out of their own being so that they become lost in him. Such as they are, however, these people become the wonder and admiration of others. God gives them gifts upon gifts, graces upon graces—visions, revelations, inward voices, ecstasies, and so on. It appears as though God's only care is to enrich and beautify them, to tell them his secrets. All joys are theirs.

Spiritual Rivers

This does not imply that they bear no heavy crosses, no fierce temptations. These sufferings are the shadows that cause their virtues to shine with greater brilliance. They vigorously push back the temptations. They bear the crosses bravely. They even desire more of this suffering. They're all flame and fire, enthusiasm and love. God uses them to accomplish great things, and it seems as though they only need to desire a thing in order to receive it from God. He finds his delight in satisfying all their desires and accomplishing all that they will. However, there are degrees of progress in this path, and some achieve a much higher standard of holiness than others. Their danger lies in focusing upon what God has done for them, thus stopping at the gifts instead of being led by the gifts to the giver.

In giving his grace, and in the abundance with which he gives it, God's plan is to bring them closer to himself. However, they use his grace for entirely different goals. They rest in it. They reflect upon it, look at it, and appropriate

The Second River

it. From this arises vanity, self-regard, preferring themselves over others, complacence, and often the destruction of religious life.

Considered on their own, these people are admirable, and sometimes by a special grace, they are made very helpful to others, particularly if they have been saved from great depths of sin. However, they are usually less equipped to lead others than those who are described later, for being closer to God themselves, they have a fear of sin and often withdraw from sinners. Having never experienced the miseries they see in others, they're shocked and unable to offer either help or advice. They expect too much piety. They don't lead others toward it step by step. If they come into contact with weak ones, they don't help them as they are in their weakness or in accordance with God's designs — in fact, they often try to avoid them. They find it difficult to interact with those who haven't reached their own level of holiness, preferring a solitary life to the ministry of love.

Spiritual Rivers

They appear to be equal to or more advanced than the third class of souls. They use the same words—death, loss of self, self-annihilation, and so on—and it's true that they do die in their own way and that they lose themselves. In seasons of devotion, they often lose or suspend their physical perceptions. These souls are thus passive, but the light, love, and strength they have is in themselves.

People like this are so laden with goods that their progress is very slow. What must be done, then, to guide them away from this path? There is a safer and surer path for them—the path of faith. They need to guided away from the natural to the supernatural, from things that are understood and perceived as profound into the darkness of faith. It's pointless trying to decide whether these perceptible things are from God or not because they must all be left behind. If they are from God, then God will carry them forward if they will only abandon ourselves to him. This second type of people have much more

The Second River

difficulty entering the path of faith than the first type. Because what they have is so substantial and so clearly from God, they refuse to believe that there is anything higher for them in the church of God. They cling to what they have already.

So many spiritual possessions appear to be great virtues to those who are not divinely enlightened, but to those who are enlightened, they are great and dangerous shortcomings. These people follow rules and regulations, which are marked by caution, as their obedience to God. Although they appear to be dead to themselves, they remain strong and vigorous. They are indeed dead to their own desires but not to their own foundation.

Souls like these often receive an inner silence, certain descents into God, which they can perceive and explain well. However, they do not have that secret longing to be nothing, like with the third type of souls. It's true they desire to be nothing through a kind of outward annihilation, a deep humility, a reduction of self under the immense weight of God's greatness. However, this is an annihilation that they live in without being annihilated. They have the feelings of annihilation without the reality. Their souls are instead sustained by these feelings, and this condition is more satisfying to their souls than any other because it offers more assurance.

Usually death alone brings this type of soul to God—except perhaps for some privileged ones, whom God intends to be the lights of his church or whom he plans to sanctify more completely. These he strips, by degrees, of all their riches. However, few are courageous enough to be willing, after so many blessings, to lose them all, so few progress beyond this state. It may be God's will that they should not progress and that, as in the Father's house there are many rooms, they should only occupy this one. Let us leave the reasons to God.

Four

The Third River — First Stage

What can we say about the souls in this third path unless it is that they resemble rushing streams that arise from high in the mountains? Their springs are in God himself, and they don't have a moment's rest until they are lost in him. Nothing stops them. No burdens are laid upon them. They rush forward with a speed that alarms even the most confident. These rivers flow without order, here and there, wherever they can find a passage. They don't have regular channels or an orderly flow. Sometimes they become muddy by flowing through ground that

Spiritual Rivers

isn't firm, their rushing waters carrying away the soil. Sometimes they seem to be permanently lost from view. Then they appear again, but it's only to throw themselves into another gorge even deeper than the last. It is a game for these cataracts to show themselves, to lose themselves, and to break themselves against the rocks. Their progress is so rapid it can hardly be observed.

Finally, after many waterfalls and deep gorges, after smashing against rocks, after being lost and found many times over, they reach the sea, and there they are lost and never found again. However poor, shabby, impractical, and lacking in goods this poor river might have been, it is wonderfully enriched in the sea. It's not rich with its own riches like the other rivers, which can only carry a certain amount of goods and certain treasures. It's rich with the riches of the sea itself. It bears in its arms the largest ships. It is the sea that bears those ships, of course, but it is also the river, for the river has become one with the sea.

The Third River — First Stage

This rushing river doesn't lose its nature when it flows into the sea—even though it is so changed and lost in the sea that it cannot be recognized. It will always remain what it was, but its identity is lost, not in terms of existence but in terms of quality. It so takes on the qualities of salt water that it retains no qualities of its own. The more it loses itself and remains in the sea, the more it exchanges its own nature for that of the sea.

Happy loss, who can describe you? Who can describe what this good-for-nothing river has gained? It was despised and seen as a mad thing. The smallest boat could not be trusted on it because the river, unable to restrain itself, would have dragged the boat with it. What do you say about the fate of this rushing river, you great rivers who flow with such majesty, who are the delight and admiration of the world, and who take pride in the quantity of goods you carry? What has become of this poor stream, which you regarded with contempt or at best with

Spiritual Rivers

compassion? What work can it do now — or rather, what work can it *not* do? You are now its servants. The riches that you possess are only the overflow of its abundance.

Before discussing the happiness of a soul that is thus lost in God, however, we must begin with its origins and then move forward by degrees.

As I've said, the soul, having proceeded from God, has a continual inclination to return to him. Just as God is its starting point, he is also its final destination. The human heart can find no rest until it returns to its origin and its center, which is God. It is like fire, which moves outward continuously once it escapes its boundaries and does not rest until it is returned to them. Then, by a miracle of nature, the same fire that consumed everything with its actions is perfectly at rest. Poor souls who seek happiness in this life, you will never find it apart from God. Seek instead to return to God. In him, all your longings and troubles, your uneasiness and anxiety, will be reduced to perfect rest.

The Third River — First Stage

As fire nears its center, it always comes to rest even though its intensity increases. It is the same with the soul. As the soul nears God, its speed increases and, at the same time, it becomes more peaceful. Its rest—or rather its peace, since it is not at rest but is pursuing a peaceful course—increases so that its peace increases its speed, and its speed increases its peace. The hindrances arise from sins and human imperfections. For a time, they hold the soul back—more or less, depending on the magnitude of the fault.

The soul is then aware of its actions, in the same way that fire, when it encounters obstacles such as pieces of wood or straw, ceases to move on in order to stop and consume these obstacles. The larger the obstacle, the more its activity increases. If the obstacle is a piece of wood, longer and stronger activity is required to consume it, but if the obstacle is only a straw, it's burned up in a moment and only slightly slows the fire's progress. The obstacles that the

Spiritual Rivers

fire encounters only give it new energy to overcome everything that slows it from returning to its rest. The more obstacles the fire encounters, and the more considerable they are, the more they will slow its progress. If it continually meets new obstacles, it will be held back and prevented from ever returning to its rest.

Those who have not sinned as indecently as others should be expected to advance more rapidly, and this is often the case. However, it seems that God takes pleasure in making "grace increase where sin has most increased." I believe that one of the reasons for this can be found in the way that those who have not sinned regard their own righteousness. That self-regard can become an obstacle more difficult to overcome then even the most indecent sins because we cannot be as attached to sins that are so hideous in themselves as we can be to our own righteousness. God, who will do no violence to liberty, leaves such hearts to enjoy their holiness at their own pleasure. Meanwhile, he finds his pleasure

The Third River — First Stage

in purifying the most miserable. To accomplish his purpose, he sends a stronger and fiercer fire to consumes those base sins more quickly than a slower fire will consume smaller obstacles.

It even appears that God loves to set his throne in these criminal hearts in order to better manifest his power, showing that he can restore the disfigured soul to its original condition and make it even more beautiful than it was before it fell. Those who have sinned much are conscious of a great fire consuming all their sins and hindrances. They often find their way blocked by attacking sins, but this fire consumes those sins, again and again, until they are completely overcome. As the fire goes on consuming, the obstacles are more and more easily overcome. By the end, the obstacles are no more than straws, and far from slowing its progress, they only make the fire burn more fiercely.

Next, let us consider the soul in its original state and then follow it though its various stages—if God, who inspires these thoughts

Spiritual Rivers

that occur to me as I write, wills that we should do so.

Because God's plan for the soul is that it should become lost in him in a way that ordinary Christians do not understand, he begins his work by giving the soul a sense of its distance from him. As soon as the soul has perceived and experienced this distance, the natural inclination that it has to return to its source — an inclination that has been deadened by sin — is revived in the soul. The soul experiences true sorrow for sin. It is painfully conscious of the evil that this separation from God causes. These feelings lead the soul to seek the means of freeing itself from this troubling situation and entering into the sure rest that it can see from afar. However, that great distance only increases the soul's anxiety and its longing to pursue that rest until it finds it.

Some of those who are thus enlivened have never been taught that they must seek to have God within themselves and not expect to find

The Third River — First Stage

him in outward righteousness. Therefore, they give themselves to intellectual contemplation and search outwardly for what can only be found within. They seldom succeed in this study because God, who has better things in mind for them, does not allow them find any rest in it. It only serves to increase their longing. Their wound is within the heart, and when they lay an external bandage over it, that bandage only serves to foster the disease instead of healing it. They struggle a long time with this work, and their struggling merely increases their powerlessness. Unless God, who takes their care upon himself, sends some messenger to show them a different way, they will waste their time and continue wasting it for as long as they remain unassisted.

However, God is abundant in his goodness. He never fails to send them help, although it may be passing and temporary. As soon as they are taught that they cannot advance because their wound is inward and they are trying to heal it with outward methods, they are led to seek

Spiritual Rivers

in the depths of their own hearts for what they have sought in vain outside of themselves. Then they discover—with an overwhelming astonishment—that they have within themselves the treasure that they have been seeking for in distance places. Then they rejoice in their new freedom. They marvel that prayer is no longer a burden. The more they retreat within themselves, the more they taste a certain mysterious *something* that overwhelms them and carries them away. They desire to always love like this and be buried within themselves.

However, what they experience, delightful as it seems, does not stop them but leads them to continue on toward something greater that they have not yet discovered. Now they are filled with love and energy. They seem to already be in Paradise because what they now possess within themselves is infinitely sweeter than all the joys of earth. They can leave those pleasures behind without any pain. They would abandon the whole world to enjoy for one hour their present

The Third River — First Stage

experience. Prayer has become their continual disposition. Their love increases day by day so that their only desire is to always love and never be interrupted.

Because they are not yet strong enough to be undisturbed by outward interactions, they shun and fear them. They love to be alone and enjoy the caresses of their beloved. They have within themselves a counselor who allows them to find no pleasure in earthly things. He doesn't allow them to commit a single sin without making them feel, through his coldness, how much sin displeases him. This coldness from God in times of sinning is for them the most terrifying punishment. It seems that God's only concern is to correct and reprove them, that his only goal is their improvement. It is a surprise to themselves and to others that through this method they change more in a month—or even in a day—than they did in several years through their studies. God, it belongs to you alone to correct and purify the hearts of your children.

Spiritual Rivers

When the soul is further advanced in this holy life, God has another way of purifying the soul. He reveals himself more fully to the soul when it falls. Then the soul is filled with confusion. It would rather suffer the most severe punishment after it has sinned than to experience this goodness of God.

These people become so filled with their own feelings that they want to give the same to others. They long to teach the whole world to love God. Their feelings for him are so deep, so pure, and so disinterested that those who hear them speak—if they are not divinely enlightened—suppose that they have attained the height of perfection. Their good works are fruitful. There is no reasoning here. There is nothing but a deep and burning love. The soul feels itself seized and held tightly by a divine power that overwhelms and consumes it. They are like intoxicated people who are so possessed by wine that they don't know what they are doing and are no longer masters of themselves. If they try to study, the book falls from

The Third River — First Stage

their hands. A single line satisfies them. They can barely get through a page in a whole day, however diligently they devote themselves to it, because a single word from God awakens that hidden instinct that animates and ignites them.

Love closes their mouths and their eyes. They can't say verbal prayers because they're unable to articulate them. A heart that isn't used to this doesn't understand what it means because it has never experienced anything like it before. It doesn't understand why it cannot pray, yet it cannot resist the power that overcomes it. The heart cannot be troubled or fearful about doing wrong because the one who holds it tightly doesn't allow it to doubt that he is the one who holds it. It cannot strive against his hold because if it makes an effort to pray, it feels that he who possesses it closes its lips and compels it, with a sweet and loving forcefulness, to be silent. People might still resist him and with a strong effort speak their prayers, but besides doing harm to themselves, they lose this divine peace

Spiritual Rivers

and feel themselves drying up. They must allow themselves to be acted upon by God as he desires and not in their own ways.

The soul in this state imagines itself to exist in an inward silence because God's work within the soul is so gentle, so easy, and so quiet that the soul does not perceive it. It thinks that is has reached the summit of perfection, and it sees nothing before it but the enjoyment of the wealth it possesses.

These Christians, so enthusiastic and so desiring for God, begin to rest in this condition of enjoyment. Gradually and imperceptibly, they begin to lose the loving work of seeking God that characterized them before. They become so satisfied with their joy that they substitute the joy for God himself. This rest would thus be an irreparable loss for them if God, in his infinite goodness, did not draw them forward from this first stage and lead them into a more advanced one. Before speaking about that, however, we will look at the problems of this first stage.

Five

Problems of the First Stage

The soul in the first stage of the third way can and does make great advances, traveling from love to love and from cross to cross. However, it falls so frequently and is so selfish that it may be said that it moves only at a snail's pace even though it seems—to itself and to others—to advance infinitely. The river in this stage is in a flat country. It has not yet found the slope of the mountain down which it can throw itself and take a course that can never be stopped.

The faults of those in this stage are many. There is a confident self-regard, more hidden and deeply rooted than it was before they received these gifts and favors from God. There is a secret

Spiritual Rivers

contempt for others whom they see so far behind themselves, a harshness toward sin and sinners, like the zeal of John prior to the arrival of the Holy Spirit, when he wanted to call down fire from heaven to consume the Samaritans. There is an overconfidence in their own security and virtue. There is a hidden pride that causes them to grieve especially over the sins that they commit in public. They appropriate the gifts of God and treat them as though they were their own. Because of the strength they now possess, they forget about weakness and poverty, losing all self-distrust.

Although we will find all of this and much more in persons in this stage, they themselves are unaware of it. However, these faults make themselves known in time. Because the grace that they feel so strongly in themselves assures them that they have nothing to fear, they allow themselves to speak without being divinely commissioned. They are anxious to explain what they experience to everyone else. It's true that

Problems of the First Stage

they are useful to others because their burning words take hold of the hearts of those who hear them. However, they can't accomplish the good that they desire because God has not yet desired them to give to others what they have received. They are giving away what they themselves need at this stage—not from their abundance.

They thus exhaust themselves, as you see with the tiers of basins under a fountain. Only the fountain itself gives out of its abundance. The basins below the fountain merely give to each other from the fullness that is given to them. If the fountain is turned off, the basins no longer overflow. They are cut off from the source and dry up. This is precisely what happens to people at this stage. They want to constantly send out their waters, and it's not until it's too late that they understand that the water they were given was only for themselves, that they are not in a condition to share it because they are not connected to the source. They are like bottles of perfume that are left open. They find

Spiritual Rivers

so much sweetness in the aroma they emit that they do not perceive the loss they sustain.

They appear to practice virtue without any effort because they are filled with a general love, without reason or cause. If you ask them what they do during the day, they tell you that they love, but if you ask why they love, they tell you that they don't know. They only know that they love and that they burn with desire to suffer for the object of their love. If you ask if it is the idea of the suffering of their beloved that fills them with this desire to suffer with him, they reply that the thought of his suffering doesn't even enter their minds. Nor do they desire to imitate the virtues that they see in him because they don't think of those virtues. The sight of his beauty doesn't fill them with joy because they don't look at it. They only feel a deep wound in the depths of their hearts, but the wound is so delightful that they rest in their pain.

They find pleasure in their sorrow. They believe that they have now arrived at the consummation

Problems of the First Stage

of everything. Although they are full of the faults I have mentioned—and many others still more dangerous that are better perceived in the following stage—they rest in their imagined holiness, stopping at the means, which they mistake for the end. They would remain stationary if God did not bring the river, which at this stage is like a peaceful lake on a mountaintop, to the brow of the hill in order to send it downward, to put it on a course that will be more or less rapid, according to the depth of its fall.

It seems to me that even the most advanced in this stage have a habit of concealing their faults, both from themselves and from others. They always find excuses and justifications—not willfully but out of a certain love of their own excellence, a habitual self-deception in which they hide themselves. The faults that cause them the deepest concern are the ones that are the most noticeable to others. They have a hidden love of self, which is stronger than ever, a respect for their own position, a secret desire to attract

Spiritual Rivers

attention, a feigned modesty, and an readiness to judge others.

They also have a preference for private devotion over domestic duties, which makes them the cause for many of the sins of those around them. This is very important. The soul, feeling itself drawn so strongly and sweetly, desires to always be alone and in prayer. This causes two evils. First, in its seasons of greatest freedom, it spends too much time in solitude. Second, when the strength of love is exhausted, as it often is in this stage, it lacks that same strength during dry times. It finds it difficult to remain in prayer for long and readily shortens the time. Its thoughts wander to outward things. It is then discouraged and disheartened, thinking that all is lost, and it does everything in its power to restore itself to the presence and favor of God.

If these people were strong enough to live a balanced life, without trying to do more in times of abundance than in times of barrenness, they would satisfy everyone. As it is, they

Problems of the First Stage

are troublesome to everyone around them. They cannot humble themselves before others but think it is a gift for them to present themselves for the satisfaction of others. They preserve an austere silence when it is unnecessary, and at other times, they talk incessantly of the things of God. A wife has pangs of conscience about pleasing her husband, entertaining him, walking with him, or seeking to amuse him, but she has none about speaking uselessly for two hours with religious devotees. This is a horrible abuse. We ought to be diligent in the doing of all our duties, whatever they may be. Even if they cause us some inconvenience, we will still find great profit in doing this — not in the way we imagine, perhaps, but in hastening the crucifixion of self.

It even seems as if our Lord demonstrates that such sacrifice is pleasing to him by the grace that he pours out on it. I knew a lady who, when playing at cards with her husband in order to please him, experienced a kind of deep and intimate communion with God that she had never

Spiritual Rivers

felt in times of prayer—and it was the same with everything she did at her husband's desire. However, if she neglected these things for other duties that she thought were better, she became aware that she was not walking in the will of God. This did not prevent her from often erring in this way, however, because the attractions of contemplation and the happiness of devotion, which she preferred to these apparent wastes of time, unconsciously draw the soul away and lead it on a different path, which most people look upon as holiness. However, those who are to be taught the way of faith are not allowed to remain in those errors for long. Because God has plans to lead them on to better things, he makes them aware of their weakness.

It often happens, too, that through this death to self, and contrary to their natural inclinations, people feel themselves drawn more strongly toward their inward rest. It is natural for people to desire more strongly the things that are more difficult to obtain—and to desire most intensely

Problems of the First Stage

those things that they most earnestly try to avoid. This difficulty of being able to enjoy only a partial rest increases the rest. It causes people, even in the midst of their work, to feel themselves acted upon so powerfully that they seem to have two souls within them, the inward soul being infinitely stronger than the outward soul. However, if they leave their work in order to give that time to devotion, they find that devotion becomes an empty form, and all its joy is lost. By "devotion," I don't mean compulsory prayer, which is followed as a duty that must not be avoided, and by "work," I don't mean labors of their own choosing but the duties God has given them.

If people have spare time at their disposal, then by all means, let them spend it in prayer. They must not take upon themselves unnecessary burdens, either, and call them obligations. When the thirst for meditation is very great, the soul does not usually fall into these last-named errors but into that former one, that of retreating from the world.

Spiritual Rivers

I knew a person who spent more time in prayer when it was painful to her, struggling against disinclination, than when she experienced it as a delight. However, this is harmful to one's health because of the harm that it does to the senses and the understanding. Unable to concentrate upon any one object and deprived of the sweet communion that formerly held them in submission to God, they endure such torment that they would rather suffer the greatest trial than the violence that is required for them to focus their thoughts on God. The person I mention sometimes spent two or three hours in this painful devotion, and she has assured me that the harshest austerities would have been delightful to her compared to those times. Because a violence as strong as this in subjects so weak is sure to ruin both body and mind, I think it's better to not in any way regulate the time spent in prayer according to our wavering emotions.

The painful barrenness that I have spoken about only belongs to the first stage of faith, and

Problems of the First Stage

it's often the effect of exhaustion. Even so, those who have passed through it imagine themselves dead. They write and speak about it as the most sorrowful part of the spiritual life. It's true that they haven't known the opposite experience, and often they lack the courage to endure because in this sorrow, the soul feels deserted by God as he withdraws his perceptible support. This sorrow, however, is only caused by the senses. Having been accustomed to see and feel the goodness of God, and having never yet experienced a similar deprivation, they fall into despair, but this despair does not last long. The strength of the soul is not in any condition to bear such pressure for long. It will either turn back to look for spiritual food, or else it will give up.

This is why the Lord never fails to return quickly. Sometimes he doesn't even allow the prayer to end before he reappears. If he does not return during the hour of prayer, he comes back in a more obvious way during the day. It's as if he repents of the suffering he caused to the

Spiritual Rivers

soul of his beloved, or that he would pay back with high interest what the soul has suffered for his love.

If this consolation lasts for many days, it becomes painful. The soul calls him sweet and cruel. She asks him if he has only wounded her that she may die. But the kind lover laughs at her pain and applies a balm to her wound so sweet that she could ask to continually receive fresh wounds so that she might always find a new delight in a healing that not only restores her former health but brings an even more abundant health.

Up to this time, it has only been a game of love, and the soul would easily become used to it if her beloved did not change his actions. You poor hearts who complain about the coming and going of love, you don't understand that this is only a play, an experiment, a small taste of what will follow. The hours of absence will mark the days, the weeks, the months, and the years. You must learn to be generous at your

Problems of the First Stage

own expense, to allow your beloved to come and go as he pleases.

I see young brides who are at the height of grief when their beloved leaves them. They mourn his absence as if it were death, and they try, as far as they can, to prevent his departure. This love appears to be deep and strong, but it is not so by any means. The pleasure they derive from the sight of their beloved is what they mourn. They seek their own satisfaction. If they sought the pleasure of their beloved, they would rejoice in the pleasure that he finds away from them as much in as the pleasure that he finds with them.

Theirs is self-interested love, but it doesn't appear so to them. On the contrary, they believe that they only love him for what he is. It is true, poor souls, that you do love him for what he is, but you love him because of the pleasure you find in what he is. You reply that you are willing to suffer for your beloved. True — provided that he will be the witness and the companion of

Spiritual Rivers

your suffering. You say you desire no rewards for your suffering. I agree, but you do desire that he knows about your suffering and that he approves of it.

Is there anything more plausible than the desire that the one for whom we suffer should know it, approve of it, and take delight in it? Oh, how wrong your reasoning is! Your jealous lover will not permit you to enjoy the pleasure that you take from seeing his satisfaction with your sorrow. You must suffer without his appearing to see it, approve it, or even know about it. That would be too gratifying. What pain we would suffer on those conditions, knowing that our beloved sees our woes and takes an infinite pleasure in them. This is too great a pleasure for a generous heart. However, I am sure that the greatest generosity of those in this stage never goes beyond this.

It doesn't belong to this stage but the next for us to suffer without our beloved being aware of it. In the next stage, he seems to despise what

Problems of the First Stage

we do to please him and turn away from it. He seems to scorn what formerly charmed him. He seems to repay what we do for him alone with a terrible coldness and distance, to answer our pursuit of him with abandonment. Without complaint, we lose everything that he had given as pledges of his love, everything that we think we have repaid with our love, our faithfulness, and our suffering. Not only do we allow ourselves to be robbed in this way, but without complaining, we allow others to be enriched with our treasures, never ceasing to do what do what would please our absent lover, never ceasing to follow after him.

If through unfaithfulness or distraction we stop for a moment, we then double our speed without fearing or even thinking about the dangers. We may fall a thousand times—until we are so weary that we lose our strength and die from endless fatigue. If, perhaps, our beloved turns and looks upon us, his glance restores life through the exquisite pleasure it gives, but

Spiritual Rivers

in the end, he becomes so cruel that he lets us die for lack of help. All of this, as I've said, does not belong to this first stage but to the one that follows. I must say here, though, that this first stage lasts a very long time unless God desires the soul to make great advances. And as I have said, many never move beyond it.

Six

The Third River — Second Stage

Having come to the brow of the hill, this third type of river enters the second stage of the passive way of faith. This soul, which was resting so peacefully on the mountaintop, had no thought of leaving it. However, lacking downward slope, these waters of Heaven became tainted by their lingering on earth. There is a difference between stagnant waters that have no outlet and moving waters that have an outlet. The former, with the exception of the sea and those large lakes that resemble the sea, grow putrid. Their lack of motion causes their destruction. The latter, after leaving their source,

Spiritual Rivers

have an easy outlet, and the more rapidly they flow, the more they are preserved.

As soon as God gave this soul the gift of passive faith, he also gave it an instinct to seek him as its center. In its unfaithfulness, the soul stifles this instinct to seek God in order to enjoy its rest. It would remain stationary if God did not revive this instinct by bringing the soul to the edge of the mountain, where it is forced to hurl itself downward.

At first, the soul is aware of having lost the calmness it expected to have forever. Its waters, formerly so tranquil, begin to be noisy. Its waves are disturbed. They run and crash over each other. Where do the waters run to? They seem to run toward their own destruction. If they had the power to desire anything, they would restrain themselves and return to their former calm, but that is impossible. The precipice is there. They must fall from slope to slope.

The water—that is, the soul—always reappears in this stage. It's embattled and thrown

The Third River — Second Stage

downward. One wave follows another, and the other takes it up and smashes it with its falling. However, this water still finds certain flat places on the slope of the mountain where it takes a little relaxation. It delights in the clearness of its waters, and it sees that its falls and the breaking of its waves against the rocks have made it more pure. It finds itself delivered from its noise and storms. It thinks that it has now found its resting place, and it believes this all the more readily because it cannot doubt that the stage through which it has just passed has greatly purified it. It sees that its waters are clearer, and it no longer smells of the disagreeable odor that certain stagnant places had given it on the top of the mountain. It's even acquired a certain insight into its own condition. It has seen by the disturbed state of its passions — the waves — that these passions were not lost but only asleep.

Just as the river thought that it had lost its way when it was falling down the mountain on its way to this level place, without any hope of

Spiritual Rivers

recovering its lost peace, so it forgets that former trouble now that it no longer hears the smashing of its waves. It finds itself flowing calmly and pleasantly along the sand, and it never imagines there will be a return of those troubles. It sees that it has a fresh purity. It doesn't fear that it will again become soiled, for it is not stagnant here but flows on as gently and brightly as possible. Ah, poor river, you think that you've found your resting place and are firmly established in it. You begin to delight in your own waters. The swans glide upon them and rejoice in their beauty.

But how surprised you will be when, as you flow along so happily, you suddenly encounter a slope longer and more dangerous than the first. Then the river falls back into its upheaval. Before, it was only a moderate noise. Now the noise is unbearable. The river falls with a crash and a roar greater than ever. It can hardly be said to have a bed, for it falls from rock to rock, crashing downward without order or reason. It alarms everyone with its noise. They all fear to approach it. Poor

The Third River — Second Stage

river! What will you do? In your fury, you scour away everything in your path. You feel nothing but the descent that hurries you downward. You think you are lost. But no, do not fear. You are not lost, but the time of your happiness is not yet arrived. There must be many more disturbances and losses. You have only just started on your way.

In time, this crashing river senses it has reached the foot of the mountain and another level place. It resumes its former calm—an even deeper one—and after having gone through possibly years of these changes, it enters the third stage. However, before speaking about the third stage, I will touch upon the condition of those who enter this second stage and the first steps on this path.

After spending some time in the peacefulness of the first stage, the soul thinks that it has acquired all the virtues in their full extent and that all its passions are dead. It expects to enjoy, with the greatest safety, a happiness that it has no fear of losing. The soul is then astonished to find that, instead of climbing higher or at least

Spiritual Rivers

remaining in its present position, it comes to the slope of the mountain. To its amazement, it begins to notice an inclination for the things it had given up. It sees its deep calm suddenly disturbed. Distractions come in crowds, one upon another. The soul finds only stones in its path, dryness and aridity. A feeling of distaste comes into prayer. Its passions, which the soul thought were dead, all revive.

The soul is completely astonished at this change. It would like to return to the top of the mountain or at least to remain where it is, but this cannot be. The downward plunge is there, and the soul must fall, not into sin but into a deprivation as in the prior stage. It does its best to get up after it falls. It does everything in its power to restrain itself, to cling to some devotional practices. It makes an effort to return to its former peace. It seeks solitude in the hope of recovering it. But all its labors are for nothing. It longs to make things right but finds no way of doing so. The river must go on its way. It drags

The Third River — Second Stage

with it everything that opposes it. Seeing that it no longer finds support in God, it looks for support in itself and others, but it finds none, and its unfaithfulness only increases its fearfulness.

At last, the poor bride, not knowing what to do, weeping everywhere over the loss of her beloved, is filled with astonishment when he again reveals himself to her. At first, she is charmed at the sight because she feared she had lost him forever. She's all the more happy because she finds he has brought with him new wealth, a new purity and a great distrust of self. She no longer has the desire to stop as she did before. She flows on continuously, though peacefully and gently. But she still trembles with the fear that she might again lose the treasure that is all the more precious to her because she had so deeply felt its loss. She fears she might displease him and that he will leave her again. She tries to be more faithful to him and to not make an end of the means.

However, this rest carries away the soul, overwhelms it, and makes it idle. The soul cannot

Spiritual Rivers

help being aware of its peace, and it desires to always be alone. It has again acquired a spiritual greediness. To rob it of solitude is to rob it of life. The soul is more selfish than before because what it owns has become more delightful. It seems to be in a new rest, moving along calmly, when all at once it comes to another descent, steeper and longer than the former one. It tries to hold itself back — but in vain. It must fall. It must crash downward from rock to rock.

The soul is astonished to find that it has lost its love for prayer and devotion. It does violence to itself by trying to continue. It only finds death at every step. Everything that used to revive the soul is now the cause of this death. The soul's peace is gone, leaving disturbance and problems that are greater than ever. This is caused by passions, which come back to life with more strength because they'd appeared to be extinct, and by suffering, which the soul has no strength to bear. The soul arms itself with patience. It weeps, groans, and is troubled. The bride

The Third River — Second Stage

complains that her beloved has forsaken her, but her complaints are not heeded. Life becomes death to her. All that is good she finds difficult, with an inclination towards evil that draws her away. Having tasted the creator, she can find no rest in the creature. She crashes on more violently. The steeper the rocks and the greater the obstacles, the more she increases her speed.

The soul is like the dove from the ark, which finding no rest for the sole of its foot, was forced to return. But what could the poor dove have done if, when it desired to re-enter the ark, Noah had not put out his hand to bring it in? It could only have fluttered about the ark, seeking rest but finding none. So this poor dove flutters about the ark until the divine Noah, having compassion for her distress, opens the door and receives her to himself. Oh, wonderful and loving method of the goodness of God! He only eludes the searching of the soul in order to make it fly to him more quickly. He hides himself so that he will be sought. He appears to let her fall

Spiritual Rivers

so that he will have the joy of sustaining her and lifting her up.

You strong and lively ones who have never experienced these artifices of love, these apparent jealousies, these flights that are so lovely for the souls who have passed through them but are so terrifying for those who experience them—you don't know these absences of love because you are satisfied by the abiding presence of your beloved. If he hides himself, it is for a short enough time that you can't judge the joy of his presence by the pain of a long absence. You've never experienced your own weakness and your need of his help. However, those who are forsaken in this way learn to depend no longer on themselves but only on the beloved. His trials have made his gentleness more necessary for them.

These people often commit sins through sheer weakness. Because they're deprived of all perceptible support and because these sins fill them with such shame, they would hide themselves from their beloved if they could. In the

The Third River — Second Stage

terrible confusion into which they are thrown, he gives them a glimpse of himself. He touches them with his scepter, like another Ahasuerus, so that they will not die. At other times, with his severity, he makes them aware of how much their unfaithfulness displeases him. If they could sink into dust, they would. They would do anything to repair the injury done to God. If by any slight neglect, which seems like a crime to them, they have offended their neighbor, they would be willing to make any repayment.

It is pitiful to see the condition of the one who has driven away her beloved. She never stops running after him, but the faster she goes, the further he seems to leave her behind. If he stops, it's only for a moment so she can catch her breath. She thinks that she must die now because she no longer finds life in anything. It has all become death to her — prayer, reading, discussion. It's all dead. She loses the joy of service — or rather, she dies to it, performing it with so much pain and weariness that it is like death to her.

Spiritual Rivers

In the end, after having fought well but uselessly, after a long succession of conflicts and rest, of lives and deaths, she begins to see how she has abused the grace of God. She sees that this state of death is better for her than life. Seeing her beloved returning and finding that she possesses him more purely, she sees that the state that came before her rejoicing was a purification for her. She thus abandons herself willingly to death and to the coming and going of her beloved. She gives him full liberty to come and go as he chooses. She receives instruction as she is able to bear it. Little by little, she loses her joy in herself and is thus prepared for a new stage. The further the soul advances, the more its joys become short, simple, and pure, and the more its deprivations become long and agonizing. In the end, it loses its own joy and finds it no longer. This is the third stage, a stage of death, burial, and decay. This second stage ends in death and goes no further.

Seven

The Third River — Third Stage

1. The Plundering of the Soul

You have seen dying persons who, after they have been believed to be dead, have all at once assumed a new strength that they keep until their death. They are like lamps whose oil is spent. They flicker in the gathering darkness but only to die out more quickly. So the soul sends out flames that only last for a moment. It has bravely resisted death, but its oil is spent.

The sun of righteousness has so withered the soul that it's forced to die. The poor soul that

Spiritual Rivers

is burned by the sun thinks it's paralyzed, but the truth is that the torment it suffers prevents it from recognizing the nature of its pain. As long as the sun was obscured by clouds and sent out rays that were buffered, the soul felt the heat and thought it was burning. In reality, the soul was only slightly warmed. However, when the sun shone fully upon it, the soul felt itself burning without believing that it was even being warmed.

Oh, sweet and cruel love! Do you have lovers only to deceive them like this? You wound these hearts, and then you hide your arrows and make your lovers pursue what has wounded them. You attract them and show yourself to them, and when they long to possess you, you flee from them. When you see the soul reduced to the final extremity, out of breath from its continual pursuit, you show yourself for a moment so that it might regain life, only to be killed a thousand times with ever-increasing severity. Why don't you kill with a single blow? Why give wine to a dying heart and restore life in order to destroy

The Third River — Third Stage

it again? This is your game. You wound to the death, and when you see the victim on the point of expiring, you heal one wound in order to inflict another. Usually we only die once, but you take away our lives time after time. Oh life, which cannot be lost without so many deaths! Oh death, which can only be attained through the loss of so many lives!

This stage of death is extremely long, and just as I have said that very few pass through the other stages, so I say that far fewer pass through this one. Many people are astonished to see holy persons, who have lived like angels, die in terrible anguish, even despairing of their salvation. It is because they have died in this mystical death. Because God desired to encourage their advancement and because they were near their end, he increased their sorrow.

The work of stripping the soul must be left entirely to God. He will do the work perfectly, and the soul will accept the plundering and death without putting obstacles in the way. However,

Spiritual Rivers

doing the work for ourselves means turning a divine condition into a vile one. There are people who have done this plundering to themselves. They remain stationary. Because the stripping away is their own doing, God does not clothe them with himself. God's design in stripping the soul is to clothe it again. He only impoverishes so that he might enrich. He substitutes himself for everything that he takes away, but that cannot be the case for those whose plundering is their own work. They indeed lose the gifts of God, but they do not possess God himself in exchange.

In this stage, the soul's efforts to sustain itself will only be its irreparable loss because it is seeking to save a life that must be lost. A person who wants to let a lamp die out without extinguishing it only needs to stop supplying it with oil, and it would die out by itself. However, if this person continues replenishing the lamp with oil, it will never go out. It's the same with the soul in this stage. However feebly, if it comforts itself, not allowing itself to be killed, it will by those acts slow its death. Poor

The Third River — Third Stage

soul, stop fighting against death, and you will live through your death.

I seem to see a drowning man before me. He makes every effort to rise to the surface of the water. He holds on to anything that offers itself to his grasp. He preserves his life for as long as his strength holds out and is only drowned when that strength fails. It is thus with Christians. They try to prevent their deaths for as long as possible. Only the failure of all power makes them die. God, who wishes to speed this death and who has compassion upon them, cuts off the hands with which they cling to support, forcing them to sink into the deep. The more their suffering increases, the greater is their helplessness in bearing it. The most painful part of this condition is that the trouble always begins through some fault in the sufferers, who believe they have brought it upon themselves. In the end, the soul agrees that God should deprive it of the joy of his gifts, and it admits that he is just in doing so. It doesn't even hope to possess these gifts again.

Spiritual Rivers

When those in this state see others living in communion with God, their anguish is doubled, and they sink in the feeling of their own nothingness. They long to be able to imitate those others, but finding all their efforts useless, they are forced to die. In the words of the scripture, they say, "What I feared has come upon me."

"What!" they say. "To lose God, and to lose him for ever, without the hope of ever finding him again! To be deprived of love for time and for eternity! To be unable to love him whom I know is so worthy of my love!"

Isn't it sufficient, divine lover, to cast aside your bride, to turn away from her, without forcing her to lose love, as it seems, forever? She thinks she has lost love, but she has never loved more strongly or more purely. She has indeed lost the vigor, the sensible strength of love, but she has not lost love itself. On the contrary, she possesses it to a greater degree than ever. She cannot believe this, but it is easily understood because the heart cannot exist without love.

The Third River — Third Stage

In this moment, the bride of Christ is far from taking pleasure in anything. She regards the rebellion of her desires and her involuntary sin as terrible crimes that draw the hatred of her beloved. She tries to cleanse and to purify herself, but she's no sooner washed than she seems to fall into a slough more filthy and polluted than that from which she has just escaped. She doesn't see that it is because she runs that she is defiled and falls so frequently, but she is so ashamed to run in this state that she doesn't know where to hide herself. Her clothes are filthy. She loses everything she has in the race.

Her bridegroom helps to ruin her for two reasons. First, he does so because she has soiled her beautiful garments with her vain indulgences and has appropriated the gifts of God in thoughts of self-regard. Second, he does so because in running, her path will be blocked by this burden of self-appropriation. Even the fear of losing such riches would decrease her speed.

Spiritual Rivers

Poor soul, what have you become? Before, you were the delight of your bridegroom. He took such pleasure in adorning and beautifying you. Now you are so naked, so ragged, and so poor that you don't dare to look at yourself or appear before him. Those who look at you now, having so much admired you in the past and seeing you now so marred, believe that either you have gone mad or have committed a great crime that's caused your beloved to abandon you. They don't see that this jealous husband desires that his bride should be his alone. He sees that she is amusing herself with her ornaments, that she delights in them, that she is in love with herself, that she sometimes ceases looking at him in order to look at herself, and that her love to him is growing cold because her self-love is so strong. Seeing this, he is strips her and takes her beauty and riches away before her eyes.

In the abundance of her wealth, she delights in considering herself. She sees good qualities in herself that attract her love and divert it from

The Third River — Third Stage

her bridegroom. In her foolishness, she doesn't see that she is only made fair by the beauty of her beloved and that if he removed it, she would be so hideous that she would be frightened of herself. More than this, she neglects to follow him wherever he goes. She worries that she might spoil her complexion or lose her jewels.

Jealous love, how good that you come to discipline this proud one, to take what you have given her, so that being naked and destitute, nothing will slow her journey. Thus our Lord strips the soul, little by little, robbing her of her ornaments, gifts, positions, and favor—that is, of all that she perceives and consciously possesses—which are like jewels that weigh her down. Then he takes away her natural capacity for good works, which are her clothes. After that, he destroys her personal beauty, removing divine virtue, and she finds divine virtue impossible to practice.

The bride sees that her husband takes from her, little by little, the riches he had given to her. At first, she is greatly troubled by this loss, but

Spiritual Rivers

what troubles her most is not so much the loss of her riches as the anger of her beloved. She thinks that he takes back his gifts in anger. She sees how she has abused them, the pleasure she has taken in them, and it so fills her with shame that she is ready to die of embarrassment. She lets him do as he pleases and does not dare say, "Why do you take away what you have given to me?" She sees that she deserves this and looks on in silence.

Though she keeps silent, it is not so profound a silence now as it will be afterwards. Her silence is broken by sobs and sighs. When she looks at her bridegroom, she's astonished to find that he appears to be angry with her for weeping over his justice towards her and for thinking so little of her abuse of those gifts. She tries then to let him know that she doesn't care about the loss of his gifts — if only he will stop being angry with her. She shows him her tears and her grief at having displeased him. She's so aware of the anger of her beloved that she no longer thinks about her lost riches.

The Third River — Third Stage

After allowing her to weep for a long time, her lover appears to be appeased. He consoles her, and with his own hand, he dries her tears. What a joy it is, then, for her to see this new goodness of her beloved after what she has done. He doesn't restore her former riches, and she doesn't long for them. She is only too happy to be looked upon, consoled, and caressed by him. At first, she receives his caresses with so much embarrassment that she dares not to lift her eyes. But then, forgetting her past sorrow in her present happiness, she loses herself in the new caresses of her beloved. Thinking no more of past misery, she relishes and rests in these caresses, and in this way, she compels the bridegroom to again be angry and to ruin her once more.

God strips away the riches of the soul little by little. The weaker the souls are, the longer the stripping away continues. The stronger they are, the sooner it is completed because God takes away more things at once and more often. But however brutal this treatment may be, it

Spiritual Rivers

only concerns the outer superficialities — that is, gifts, graces, and favors. This guiding of God is so wonderful, the result of such deep love to the soul, that it would never be believed except by those who have experienced it. The heart is so full of itself, so permeated with self-regard, that if God did not treat it like this, it would be lost.

Some might ask, "If the gifts of God produce such evil consequences, then why are they given?" Out of this abundant goodness, God gives these gifts in order to draw the soul away from sin — from attachment to created things — and bring it back to himself. He gives these gifts to wean the soul from earth and self and to love him, at least from gratitude. However, we use these gifts to foster self-love and self-regard. And self-love is so deeply rooted in people that these gifts only increase it. We find new charms in ourselves that we had not before discovered. We delight in them and appropriate to ourselves what belongs only to God. It is true, God could

The Third River — Third Stage

rescue us from this, but for reasons of his own, he does not do so.

The soul whose riches are stripped away by God begins to see that it was not so rich as it imagined, that all its virtue was in Christ. It sees that it has abused his grace, and it agrees that he should take back his gifts. The bride says, "I will be rich with the riches of my bridegroom, and even though he keeps them, they will still be mine because of my union with him in heart and will." She is even glad to lose these gifts of God. She finds herself unencumbered, better suited for walking. Gradually, she becomes accustomed to this deprivation. She knows that it has been good for her. She no longer grieves because of it, and because is she is now beautiful in this way, she is content to know that she will please her bridegroom more through her natural beauty and her simple garments than she could have with all her ornaments.

Spiritual Rivers

2. The Second Stage of the Plundering of the Soul

The poor bride is always hoping to live in peace in spite of her loss. She clearly sees the good to her that has resulted from it. She sees the harm that she had done to herself through the bad use she had made of the gifts that have now been taken from her. So she is completely astonished to find that the bridegroom, who had only given her temporary peace because of her weakness, comes with even greater violence to tear her clothing from her. Poor bride, what will you do now? This is far worse than before because she needs this clothing, and it's against all decency for her to allow herself to be stripped of it. She resists with all her strength. She gives all the reasons why her bridegroom shouldn't leave her naked like this. She tells him it will bring shame upon herself.

"I have lost all the virtues that you have given me," she cries, "all your gifts, all the sweetness of

The Third River — Third Stage

your love! But I could at least make an outward show of virtue. I did works of charity. I prayed continually, even though you deprived me of benefits I could feel. But I cannot consent to lose all this. I was still clothed according to my position. The world still looked at me as your bride. If I lose this clothing, it will bring shame to you!"

"It doesn't matter, poor soul. You must consent to this loss as well. You do not know yourself yet. You think that your clothing is your own and that you can use it as you wish. But although I acquired it at such a great cost, you have given it back to me as if it were your repayment for the labors I have endured for you. Let it go. You must lose it."

Having done its best to keep its clothes, the soul now lets them go, little by little, and finds itself gradually ruined. Everything is now distasteful to the soul. Before, it had aversions and frustrations but with some power as well. Now all its power has been taken from it. Its strength of body and mind fails entirely. Only

Spiritual Rivers

the inclination for better things remains. This is the last piece of clothing, and it too must in the end be lost.

This loss of clothing happens gradually, and the process is extremely painful because all the while, the bride sees that it's caused by her own foolishness. She dares not speak for fear of irritating the bridegroom, whose anger is worse to her than death. She begins to know herself better, to see that she in herself is worthless and that everything belongs to her bridegroom. She begins to distrust herself, to lose her self-regard. However, she doesn't yet hate herself because although she is naked, she is still beautiful. From time to time, she casts a pitiful look towards the bridegroom, but she doesn't say a word. She's wounded by his anger. It seems to her that this plundering would be a small thing if she had not offended him and made herself unworthy to wear her bridal gowns.

If the bride was ashamed when her riches were first taken from her, the shame at her nakedness is infinitely more painful. She can't bear to

The Third River — Third Stage

appear before her bridegroom. Is she not even permitted to hide herself? No, she must appear so in public. The world begins to think less highly of her. It says, "Is this that bride who was once the admiration of angels and people? See how she has fallen!" These words increase her shame because she is well aware that her bridegroom has dealt justly with her. She does what she can to induce him to clothe her a little, but having stripped her of everything, he will do nothing because her clothes would prevent her seeing herself as she is.

It is a great shock to a soul that thinks itself far advanced towards perfection, seeing itself ruined like this all at once. It imagines that the old sins, from which it was once purged, must have returned. But it is mistaken. The secret is that the soul was so concealed by its clothing that it could not see what it was. It is a terrifying thing for a soul to be stripped in this way of the gifts and graces of God. It is impossible for anyone to understand or imagine what this is like without actually experiencing it.

Spiritual Rivers

3. THE THIRD STAGE
OF THE PLUNDERING OF THE SOUL

All this would be a small thing if the bride could retained her beauty, but the bridegroom robs her of that as well. She has been robbed of gifts, graces, and favors — her capacity for good. She has lost all good works, such as acts of charity, caring for the poor, and readiness to help others. However, she has not lost the divine virtues. At this point, however, these too must be lost, as far as their practice is concerned — or rather, as far as the *habit* of practicing them is concerned, a habit that she acquired on her own in order to appear fair to others. In reality, they are being even more strongly implanted. She loses virtue as virtue in this world but only so she may find it again in Christ.

This degraded bride becomes, as she imagines, filled with pride. She who was so patient, who suffered so easily, finds that she can suffer nothing. Her senses rebel through continual

The Third River — Third Stage

distractions. She can no longer discipline herself through her own efforts, and worse, she contracts corruption at every step. She complains to her beloved that "the watchmen found me as they went about in the city" and wounded her. I ought to say, however, that people in this condition do not sin willfully. God usually reveals to them such a deep-seated corruption within themselves that they cry with Job, "If only you would hide me in the grave and conceal me till your anger has passed!"

It must not be supposed that God actually allows the soul to fall into sin either here or at any other stage of progress. Although in their own eyes they are the most miserable sinners, they can find no specific sin of which they are guilty. They can only accuse themselves of being full of misery, of having feelings that are contrary to their desires. It is the glory of God that when he makes the soul most deeply conscious of its inward corruption, he does not allow it to fall into sin.

Spiritual Rivers

What makes the soul's sorrow so terrible is that it's overwhelmed with an awareness of the purity of God. That purity makes the smallest imperfection seem like as a horrifying sin because of the infinite distance between the purity of God and the impurity of the creature. The soul sees that it was originally created pure by God and that it has contracted not only the original sinfulness of Adam but thousands of actual sins. Its shame is greater than words can express. The reason that others despise Christians in this state is not to be found in any particular faults that are seen in them. Others despise them because they no longer show the same eagerness and faithfulness that formerly distinguished them. The greatness of their fall is judged from this change, and that judgment is a great mistake.

When I speak of corruption, decay, and so on, I mean the destruction of the old man though the central conviction and personal experience of the depth of impurity and selfishness in the heart of humans. This brings people to see

The Third River — Third Stage

themselves as separated from God, causing them to cry out with David, "I am a worm and not a man," and with Job, "Even if I wash myself with snow and cleanse my hands with lye, you will still plunge me into a pit, and my own clothes will abhor me."

It is not that this poor bride commits the sins of which she imagines herself guilty. In truth, she has never been purer. However, her senses and natural abilities, lacking support, wander away. In addition, as the speed of her race towards God increases, she forgets herself more, so it's no surprise that she dirties herself in the muddy places through which she passes. All her attention is directed towards her beloved. Although she doesn't perceive it because of her condition, she no longer thinks of herself and doesn't notice where she steps. Therefore, while she believes herself to be most guilty, she doesn't willingly commit a single sin. Her sins seem voluntary to herself, but they are instead faults of surprise, which she often doesn't see until after they are committed.

Spiritual Rivers

She cries to her bridegroom, and although he doesn't seem to take notice of her, he sustains her with an invisible hand. Sometimes she tries to do better, but then she becomes worse. The design of her bridegroom in letting her fall without wounding herself is that she should no longer depend on herself, that she should recognize her helplessness, that she should sink into complete self-despair, and that she should say with Job, "My soul chooses death rather than life." Here is where the soul begins truly to hate itself and know itself in a way that it would never have known if it hadn't passed through this experience.

All of our natural knowledge of self, however advanced it may be, is not sufficient to make us truly hate ourselves. As Jesus says, "Anyone who loves their life will lose it, while anyone who hates their life in this world will keep it for eternal life." Only an experience like this can reveal to the soul its infinite depth of wretchedness. No other way can bring true purity. If any other experience gives any revelation, it is only

The Third River — Third Stage

superficial, not in the depths of the heart, where the impurity is rooted. God searches the deepest recesses of the soul for that hidden impurity that comes from the self-regard and self-love that he plans to destroy.

Take a sponge that is full of impurities and wash it as much as you wish. You will clean the outside, but you will not make it clean throughout unless you squeeze out all the filth. This is what God does. He squeezes the soul in a painful way, but he does so to bring out all that was most deeply hidden. This is the only way for us to be radically purified. Without it, we will always be filthy even though we might outwardly appear quite clean. It is necessary for God to make the soul thoroughly aware of its true condition. Without this experience, we would never believe what human nature, left to itself, is capable of doing. Yes, our own being, abandoned to itself, is worse than all devils.

We must not believe that the soul in this state of misery has actually been abandoned by God.

Spiritual Rivers

It was never better sustained. As it were, human nature is left alone for a little while and brings all this destruction without the soul taking any part in it. This poor desolate bride, running here and there in search of her beloved, not only dirties herself seriously, as I have said, by stumbling into sins of the moment and of self-regard. She also wounds herself deeply with the thorns that get in her way. She becomes so wearied that at length she is forced to die in her pursuit from a lack of help — that is, to have no hope in herself or her own works. In this condition, the thing that produces the highest good in the soul is that God shows no pity towards it. When he wants to advance the soul, he lets it run itself to death.

If God stops for a moment, delighting and reviving the soul, it is because of the soul's weakness and so that the soul's weariness will not force it to rest. When he sees that the soul is becoming disheartened and inclined to give up the race altogether, he gazes upon the soul for a moment, and the poor bride finds herself wounded afresh

The Third River — Third Stage

by his look. She wants to tell him, "Why have you forced me to run like this? Oh, if only I could find you and see you face to face!" But when she seems to take hold of him, he flees from her again. "I sought you," she cries, "but I did not find you." Because this look from her bridegroom has increased her love, she increases her speed in order to find him. Nevertheless, the joy she felt delayed her for as long as the look lasted. This is why the bridegroom doesn't gaze upon her often — only when he sees that her courage is failing.

In this condition, the bride hates herself so much that she can hardly bear herself. She thinks that her bridegroom has good reason to treat her like he does and that his indignation is what makes him leave. She doesn't see that he leaves her so that she will run after him, nor that he allows her to be soiled so that he can purify her.

When we put iron in the fire to purify it and to purge it of its dross, it seems at first to be tarnished and blackened, but afterwards,

Spiritual Rivers

it's easy to see that it has been purified. Christ only makes his bride experience her own weakness so that she will lose all the strength and support that she has in herself and so that in her despair, he might carry her in his arms and that she might be willing to be carried. Whatever her path might be, she walks like a child. However, when she is in God and is carried by him, her progress is infinite because it is the progress of God himself.

In addition to all this degradation, the bride sees others adorned with her treasures. When she sees a holy soul, she doesn't dare approach it. She sees it wearing with all the jewels that her bridegroom has taken from her, and although she admires them, she cannot desire to have these jewels again because she's so conscious of her unworthiness to wear them. It would be profane, she thinks, to put them on a person so covered with mud and filth. Although she sees the jewels decorating others, she doesn't think that jewels are the source of their happiness. If

The Third River — Third Stage

she sees any blessedness in having them, it is only because they are tokens of the love of her beloved. When she's aware of her littleness in the presence of these others, whom she regards as queens, she doesn't understand the good that will come from this nakedness, death, and decay. Her bridegroom only unclothed her so that he himself will be her clothing. As Paul says, "Clothe yourselves with the Lord Jesus Christ." He only kills her so that he will be her life: "Now if we have died with Christ, we believe that we will also live with him."

This loss of virtue, along with the other losses, is only brought about in stages, but the apparent inclination toward evil is not willful. The evil that makes us so vile in our own eyes is really no evil at all. The things that defile these people are particular sins that only exist in the emotions. As soon as they see the beauty of a virtue, they seem to constantly fall into a contrasting vice. For example, if they love truth, they speak hastily or with exaggeration, and this makes them imagine that they lie at every

Spiritual Rivers

opportunity. In truth, though, they only speak against their feelings. The more important these virtues are, and the more strongly these people cling to them because they seem to be essential, the more forcefully these virtues are torn from them.

4. The Soul's Entrance into Mystic Death

This poor soul, after having lost all it owns, must at last lose its own life through utter self-despair, wearied to death by terrible fatigue. Prayer in this stage is extremely painful because the soul is no longer able to use its own powers, which seem to be entirely taken, and because God has taken away the sweet and profound calm that supported it. The soul no longer finds any support in the creature. It finds nothing that satisfies. It tries to abandon itself to the things that delighted it in the past, but now they

The Third River — Third Stage

offer nothing but bitterness. The soul is glad to abandon those things, with nothing to show for it but sadness at its own unfaithfulness.

The imagination goes astray entirely and is almost never at rest. The three powers of the soul—understanding, memory, and the will—gradually lose their lives so that they become entirely dead. This is painful to the soul, especially when it comes to the will. The will had enjoyed a mysterious sweetness and tranquility, and this comforted the other powers in their deadness and powerlessness. This unexplainable something that sustains the soul is the hardest loss of all, and the soul works the hardest to retain it. Because it's so fragile, this something seems all the more holy and necessary. The soul would willingly content to be stripped of the two other powers—and even of the will, so far as it is a distinct and known thing—if only this something might be left. The soul could bear all its labors if it could have within itself this evidence that it is born of God.

Spiritual Rivers

However, this too must be lost, like the rest, at least according to the soul's feelings. Then the soul enters into the powerfully felt realization of all the misery that now fills it. This is what really produces the spiritual death because whatever misery the soul might endure, if this something is not lost, the soul will not die. And if this something is lost but without the soul being aware of its misery, the soul will be supported and will not die. The soul can easily understand that it must give up all dependence upon its own feelings or upon any worldly support, but it cannot consent to lose this almost imperceptible comfort and fall from weakness into the mire. This is where reason fails. This is where terrible fears fill the heart, which seems to have only enough life to be aware of its death. It is the loss of this imperceptible support and the experience of this misery that causes death.

In times like these, we must be careful to not let our feelings be willingly led away toward created things, looking there for consolation

The Third River — Third Stage

and distraction. I say willingly because we are not capable of self-denial and self-discipline in these times. The more we deny ourselves, the more we'll be pulled in the opposite direction, like a madman who wanders about if you try to restrain him too rigorously. Self-denial is useless, and it will also slow our death. What then must we do? We must be careful to give no support to our feelings. We must let them be and let them find refreshment in innocent ways.

This only applies to this stage of development. We would be wrong to treat our feelings like this during times of strength and the active work of grace. In his goodness, our Lord himself shows us see the conduct that we should pursue. At first, he puts such pressure on our feelings that they have no freedom. They have only to desire something in order to be deprived of it. God does this so that the feelings will be drawn away from their imperfect workings and confined in the heart. By severing them outwardly, he binds them inwardly with such gentleness that it costs

Spiritual Rivers

them little to be deprived of everything. In fact, they find more pleasure in this deprivation than in possessing all things. But when our feelings are sufficiently purified, God desires to draw the soul out of itself with a different action. He allows the feelings to expand outwardly. To the soul, this appears to be a great impurity, but it happens at the right time. To try to order things otherwise would be an attempt to purify ourselves in a different way from what God desires, which would defile ourselves instead.

This does not prevent us from making mistakes in this outward development of the feelings. However, the shame that it brings and our faithfulness in responding to it is the furnace in which we are most quickly purified by most quickly dying to ourselves. It is at this point that we suddenly enter the third stage of burial and decay.

Eight

Consummation of the Third Stage

This third type of river, as we have said, has passed through every imaginable change. It has been smashed against rocks—indeed, its course has been nothing but a succession of falls from rock to rock—but it has always reappeared. We have never seen it truly lost. Now it begins to lose itself in gorge after gorge. Before, it still had a course, even though it was so steep, so jumbled, and so irregular. Now it's swallowed by even greater falls into unsearchable depths. For a long time, it disappears entirely from view. Then we perceive it slightly, but more by hearing than

Spiritual Rivers

by seeing, and then it seems to again be thrown in a deeper chasm. It falls from chasm to chasm, from waterfall to waterfall, until at last it falls into the depths of the sea.

There it is lost entirely, becoming one with the sea itself, never to be found again. After so many deaths, the soul at last expires in the arms of love, yet it doesn't even perceive those arms. As it draws near to death, the soul grows weaker, but its life, though languishing and agonizing, is still life, and "while there is life there is hope," even though death is inevitable. But as the soul expires, it loses all action, all desire, all inclination, tendency, choice, repugnance, and aversion. The river must be buried out of sight. What used to be falls have become chasms. The soul falls into a depth of misery from which there is no escape. At first, this abyss seems small, but the further the soul advances, the greater it appears to be, so that it goes from bad to worse.

After their deaths and before their burials, people are still among the living. They still have

Consumption of the Third Stage

human faces, even though these are objects of terror. In the same way, at the beginning of this stage, the soul still bears some resemblance to what it was before. A certain secret imprint of God remains in it, just as a certain animal heat remains in a dead body, gradually leaving it. The soul still practices times of devotion and prayer, but this is gradually taken away. It must lose not only prayer and every gift of God, but God himself—that is, so far as he was selfishly possessed—and not just lose him for one, two, or three years but for ever. All capacity for good and all works of virtue are taken from the soul. It's left naked and stripped of everything. The world, which used to respect it so much, begins to fear it. It's not outward sin that produces this contempt from others. It's simply a powerlessness to practice its former good works with the same capacity.

Little by little, the soul loses everything to such a degree that it is entirely impoverished. The world tramples it under foot and thinks no

Spiritual Rivers

more of it. Poor soul, you must allow yourself to be buried, covered with earth, and trampled under foot by everyone. Here the heavy crosses are borne, and they are all the heavier because others think they are deserved. God pushes you so far away that he seems determined to abandon you forever. You must be patient. You must remain in your tomb. You must see that the tomb is the only fit place for you, too, all other places being even sadder. The soul flees from others, knowing that they find it repulsive. They look at this forlorn bride as an outcast, as someone who has lost the grace of God and is only fit to be buried in the ground.

The heart endures this bitterness, but even this state would be pleasant and remaining in the tomb would be easy if it were not also necessary to decay. The old life gradually becomes corrupted now. Before, there were weaknesses and failings. Now the soul sees a depth of corruption that it's never seen before because it could not imagine the nature of its own self-regard and selfishness.

Consummation of the Third Stage

What horror the soul suffers in seeing itself decay like this. All problems, contempt, and repugnance of others no longer affect the soul. It's no longer even aware of how it's deprived of the sun of righteousness because it knows his light does not penetrate the tomb. But to feel its own corruption—the soul cannot endure it. It would rather suffer anything else.

"And yet," says the soul, "if I could decay without being seen by God, I would be content. What troubles me is the horror that the sight of my corruption must cause him."

Poor, desolate one, what can you do? One would think that it would be enough for you to bear this corruption without loving it. But now you're not even sure that you don't desire it! The soul is in darkness and can't judge whether its terrible thoughts come from itself or from the evil one. It's so conscious of its unworthiness that it consents to the loss of the felt presence of God, but it can't endure the thought that the stink of its corruption reaches even to God.

Spiritual Rivers

"Let me rot!" cries the soul. "Let me find my home in the depths of hell if only I might be kept free from sin." It no longer thinks of love because it believes itself incapable of affection. It is, in its own opinion, worse than when it was in its natural state because it has fallen into the state of corruption that belongs to a body without life.

At length, the soul grows accustomed to its corruption. It notices it less and finds it to be natural except for certain times when it is tested by various temptations whose fearful impressions cause it much anguish. Poor river, weren't you better off on the mountaintop than here? You had some slight corruption then, it is true, but now, though you flow rapidly and nothing can stop you, you pass through such filthy places, so stinking with sulfur and manure, that you carry their odors away with you.

At last the soul is reduced to a state of nothingness. It has become like a person who does not exist and never will exist. It does nothing, neither good nor ill. Formerly it thought of itself, but it

Consummation of the Third Stage

does so no longer. Any works of grace are done as if by human nature, and there is no longer either pain or pleasure. The only thing left is that its ashes remain as ashes, without the hope of ever being anything but ashes. It is utterly dead, and nothing touches it from without or from within — that is, it is no longer troubled by any sensations. Reduced to nonentity at last, there is in these ashes a seed of immortality, which lives beneath these ashes and which in due time will manifest its life. But the soul is not aware of it and never expects to be revived or raised from the dead. In this condition, the faithfulness of the soul consists of letting itself be buried, crushed, and trampled down without moving any more than a corpse would and without seeking in any way to prevent its rotting.

There are those who want to apply balm to themselves. No, leave yourselves as you are. You must know your corruption and see the infinite depth of depravity within you. To apply balm is merely trying to hide your corruption with good

Spiritual Rivers

works. Don't do it! You wrong yourselves. God can tolerate you. Why can't you tolerate yourselves? The soul that is reduced to nothingness must remain in nothingness without wishing to change its condition.

This is when the rushing river finally loses itself in the sea, never to find itself in itself again but to become one with the sea. This is when the corpse feels without feeling that it is gradually being brought back to life and takes on a new life. Yet this happens so gradually that it seems like a dream. This brings us to the last stage, which is the beginning of the holy and truly inner life. This life includes countless smaller stages in which the soul's progress will be infinite, just as this river can perpetually move out into the sea, absorbing more if its nature the longer it remains.

NINE

The Third River — Fourth Stage

When this crashing river begins to lose itself in the sea, we can easily distinguish it. Its flow remains perceptible until at length it gradually loses all form of its own, taking on the form of sea. In the same way, the soul still retains something of itself as it leaves the third stage and begins to lose itself. However, in just a short time, it loses all that had been particular to itself. The corpse that has been reduced to ashes is still dust and ashes, but if another person were to swallow those ashes, they would no longer have an identity of their own. They would form part of the person who had swallowed them. Although dead and buried, the soul has so far retained its own being. Only in this fourth stage is the soul truly taken out of itself.

Up to this point, everything has happened within the individual capacity of the creature, but now the creature is removed from its own limitations and receives infinite capacity in God himself. Just as the river, when it enters the sea, loses its own being in such a way that it keeps nothing of itself and takes on the nature of the sea—or rather, is taken out of itself to be lost in the sea—so this soul loses the human in order to lose itself in the divine. The divine becomes its being and its substance—not essentially but mystically. This river then possesses all the treasures of the sea and is as glorious now as it was poor and miserable before.

It is in the tomb that the soul begins to resume life, and the light enters imperceptibly. Then it can be truly said that "the people living in darkness have seen a great light, and on those living in the

The Third River — Fourth Stage

land of the shadow of death, a light has dawned." There is a beautiful image of this resurrection in Ezekiel 37, where the dry bones gradually assume life. There is also that other passage: "A time is coming and has now come when the dead will hear the voice of the Son of God and those who hear will live." You who are rising from the tomb, you feel within yourselves a seed of life springing up, little by little. You are astonished to find a secret strength taking hold of you. Your ashes are enlivened. You find yourself in a new country.

The poor soul, which only expected to remain at rest in its grave, receives an agreeable surprise. It doesn't know what to think. It supposes that the sun must have given it a few scattered rays through some opening or crack but that its brightness will only last for a moment. It is still more astonished when it feels this secret strength permeating its entire being and that it is gradually receiving a new life—a life that it will not lose again except through the most flagrant unfaithfulness. But this new life is not like the

Spiritual Rivers

old one. This is a life in God. It is a holy life. The soul no longer lives and works from itself. Now God lives, works, and operates in it, and this continues to increase so that the soul becomes holy with God's holiness, rich with God's riches, and loving with God's love.

The soul sees that whatever it had owned in the past had been its own possession, but now it no longer possesses but is itself possessed. It only takes this new life in order to lose it—or rather, it only lives with the life of God, and because he is the essence of life, the soul lacks nothing. What a gain it has from all its losses. It's lost the created and gained the creator. It's lost the nothing and gained the all in all. It receives all things—not in itself but in God, not to possess them but to be possessed by God. The soul's riches are immense because they are God himself. Day by day, it feels its capacity increasing to vastness. Every virtue returns to it in God.

Just as the soul was stripped and ruined by degrees, so it's enriched and enlivened by

The Third River — Fourth Stage

degrees. The more it loses itself in God, the greater its capacity becomes, just as the more that a river loses itself in the sea, the more it is enlarged, having no other limits than those of the sea. The soul becomes strong and firm. It has lost the means but found the end. This divine life becomes quite natural to the soul. Because it no longer feels itself, sees itself, or knows itself, it no longer sees or understands or distinguishes anything of God as distinct or outside of itself. It's no longer conscious of love, light, or knowledge. It only knows that God is, and it no longer lives except in God. All devotion is action, and all action is devotion — it is all the same. The soul is not partial toward anything because everything is equally God.

Before, it was necessary to practice virtue in order to do virtuous works. Now all distinctions between actions are removed. The actions have no virtue in themselves. Because everything is in God, the lowest action is equal to the highest — provided that it is ordered by God and

Spiritual Rivers

performed in his timing, because everything that might be done by human will, and not in God's plan, would have a different effect, leading the soul away from God by unfaithfulness. The soul would not be taken out of this stage or its loss but out of the divine plan that makes all things one and all things God.

So the soul is indifferent as to whether it is in one condition or another, in one place or another. It is all the same to the soul, and it allows itself to be carried along naturally. It ceases to think, wish, or choose for itself. It remains content, without worry or anxiety, no longer distinguishing its inner life or talking about it. Indeed, it can be said that the soul no longer possesses an inner life because it is no longer in itself but entirely in God. If a river were entirely permeated with the sea, having the sea within and without, above and below, on every side, it would not prefer one place to another. It would all be the same to it. In the same way, the soul does not trouble itself to seek anything or to do

The Third River — Fourth Stage

anything of its own or on its own. What does it do? Nothing—always nothing. It does what it is made to do. It suffers what it is made to suffer. Its peace is unchangeable but always natural.

The soul has entered into a new natural state, yet how entirely different this state is from the state of those who are apart from God. The difference is that it is compelled to act by God without being conscious of it. Before, it was human nature that acted. The soul now seems to do neither right nor wrong but lives satisfied, peaceful, doing what it is made to do in a steady and confident manner. God alone is its guide because in the time of loss, it lost its own will. If you were to ask it what it desires, it could not tell you. It can no longer choose for itself. All desires is gone. Having found its center, the heart loses all natural inclinations, habits, and activity in the same way that it loses all repugnance and resistance. The river no longer has any downward flow or movement. It is at rest. It has reached its destination.

Spiritual Rivers

This soul is satisfied with the satisfaction of God himself, immense and general, and without knowing or understanding what satisfies it because all feelings, desires, views, and opinions, however delicate they may have been, are taken from the soul. However, this unconsciousness is very different to that of death, burial, and decay. That was a deprivation of life, a loss of desire, a separation — the powerlessness of the dying united with the insensibility of the dead. This is an elevation of the soul above all these things, an elevation that does not remove those things but renders them useless.

In this stage, God cannot be tasted, seen, or felt because he is no longer distinct from the soul but one with it. The soul has neither inclination nor desire for anything. It experienced this in the season of death and burial it but in a very different way. In that season, it came from a loss of desire and from powerlessness, but now it's caused by fullness and abundance. In the same way, if people could live on air alone, they would

The Third River — Fourth Stage

be full without feeling their fullness or knowing how they were satisfied. They would not be empty or unable to eat or to taste. They would simply be free from all need to eat because of this satisfaction, without understanding how the air, entering through all their pores, has permeated all parts of their bodies.

The soul here is in God, who is the air that it naturally breathes, but is it no more aware of its fullness than we are of the air that we breathe. Yet it *is* full. It lacks nothing. Its peace is great, but not in the way that it was peaceful before. Before, it was a lifeless peace, a kind of tomb, from which dying breaths sometimes escaped and troubled the soul. When it was reduced to ashes, the soul was also at peace, but that was a barren peace, like that of a corpse, which would be at peace in the midst of the sea's wildest storms because it would not sense them or be troubled by them, its state of death making it unaware of everything. But now the soul is elevated, as it were, to a mountaintop, and from here it sees the

Spiritual Rivers

waves rolling and tossing without fearing their attacks—or instead, it rests at the bottom of the sea, where there is always tranquility, even while the surface is stirred. The senses may suffer their sorrows, but at the core, there is always the same, calm tranquility because the one who possesses the soul is unchanging. If the sea had no bottom, anyone falling into it would sink forever, falling to greater and greater depths of the ocean, discovering more and more of its beauties and treasures. So it is with the soul whose home is in God.

What must the soul do in order to be faithful to God? Nothing—and less than nothing. It must simply allow itself to be possessed, acted upon, and moved without resistance, remaining in this new state of nature, waiting for what every moment will bring and receiving that from God without either adding to it or taking from it. It must allow itself be led at all times and to any place, regardless of appearances or reasons, and without thinking about either. The soul must itself go naturally into all things, without

The Third River — Fourth Stage

considering what would be best or most plausible. It must remain where God has placed it, in a state of evenness and stability, without being troubled to do anything and leaving to God the responsibility of providing opportunities and doing everything for it. The soul must not do its own acts of abandonment but must simply rest where it already is in the state of abandonment that is now natural to it.

The soul is not able to act on its own in any way without being aware of unfaithfulness. It possesses all things by having nothing. It finds the ability to perform every duty, for speaking and for acting, no longer in its own way but in God's. Its faithfulness does not consist of withdrawing from all activity, like one who is dead, but in doing nothing except through the life that enlivens it. A soul in this state has no inclination of its own toward anything. It lets itself go as it is led, and beyond that, it does nothing. It cannot speak of its condition because it does not see it. Although there is much here that is

Spiritual Rivers

extraordinary, life is no longer like it was in the former stages, where the creature had a hand in it and where to a large degree it belonged to the creature. In this state, the most amazing things are perfectly natural and are done without thought. The same life that gives life to the soul also acts within and through the soul. The soul has a power over the hearts of those around it but not from itself. Because nothing belongs to the soul, the soul holds nothing back.

If the soul can say nothing about such a holy condition, it is not because it fears vanity, which no longer exits, but because what it has, while having nothing, cannot be expressed because of its extreme simplicity and purity. There are many things that are part of this state but not the center, and the soul can speak easily of these things. They are the crumbs that fall from that eternal feast that the soul has begun to enjoy. They are the sparks that prove the existence of a furnace of fire and flame. However, it is impossible to speak about the center and the end

The Third River — Fourth Stage

because the only things that can be shared are what God is desires to be written or spoken at any given moment.

Is the soul unaware of its sins, one might ask, or does it commit none? The soul does commit them and is more aware of them than ever, especially at the start of its new life. The sins committed are often more subtle and delicate than before. The soul knows them better because its eyes are open. However, it's not troubled by them. It can do nothing to rid itself of them. When the soul has been guilty of unfaithfulness or sin, it's aware of a certain cloud, but the cloud passes over without the soul itself doing anything to dispel it. Any efforts the soul might make would be useless, anyway, and would only increase the soul's impurity, making the soul deeply aware that the second stain was worse than the first.

It's not a question of returning to God because a return presupposes a departure, and if we are in God, we have only to abide in him. In the same way, when a little cloud appears in the sky, the

Spiritual Rivers

wind moves the cloud but doesn't dissipate it, but when the sun shines, it's soon dispelled. The more subtle and delicate the clouds are, the more quickly they dissipate. If we only had enough faith to never to look at ourselves, what progress we would make. The defects of this condition are certain light emotions or views of self, which are born and die in a moment — certain winds of self, which pass over the calm sea, and cause ripples. These faults are removed from us little by little and continually become more delicate.

The soul, on leaving the tomb, finds itself clothed with the inclinations of Christ. It finds these inclinations just when they are needed, without thinking of them, just as a person who possesses a hidden treasure might find it unexpectedly in the time of need. The dispositions of Christ are lowliness, meekness, submission, and the other virtues that he possessed. The soul finds that all these virtues are operating within it so easily that they seem to have become a natural part of the soul. The soul's treasure is found in

The Third River — Fourth Stage

God alone, and it draws upon it endlessly in every time of need, without in any way diminishing it. This is when the soul truly "puts on" Jesus Christ, and from now on, it is Christ who acts, speaks, and moves in the soul. He is what moves it. Those around the soul no longer inconvenience it. The heart is enlarged to contain them. It desires neither activity nor rest but only to be, moment by moment, what God makes it.

In this state, the soul is capable of infinite advancement, so I will leave it to others who are living in this state to write about it. The light has not been given to me for the higher stages, and my soul is not sufficiently advanced in God to see or understand them. All that I will add is that because of the length of the road required to arrive at God, the destination is not as quickly reached as we are apt to imagine. Even the most spiritual and enlightened souls mistake the consummation of the passive way of light and love for the consummation of this stage. In reality, it is only the beginning.

Spiritual Rivers

I must also say that what I have said regarding the mind of Christ begins as soon as we enter the path of naked faith. Although the soul in the earlier stages has no distinct vision of Christ, it still has a desire to be conformed to his image. It values the cross, lowliness, and poverty. Then this desire is lost, but a secret inclination for the same things remains, and this continually deepens and simplifies, becoming every day more intimate and more hidden. But in this fourth stage, the mind of Christ is the mind of the soul, no longer distinct from the soul but like the soul's being and its own life. Christ develops his mind without leaving the soul, and the soul develops the mind of Christ with Christ, in Christ, without leaving Christ — not as a defined thing that it knows, sees, attempts, and practices, but as something natural to it. All the actions of life, such as breathing, are done naturally without thoughts, rules, or judgment. They are done unconsciously by the person who does them. So it is with the mind of Christ in

The Third River — Fourth Stage

this stage. It continually develops, as the soul is more and transformed in him, becoming more thoroughly one with him.

Because the soul is strong with the strength of God himself, God now places upon it more and heavier crosses than before. However, they are borne divinely. Before, the cross charmed the soul. It was loved and cherished. Now the cross is not thought of but is allowed to come and go. The cross itself becomes God, like all other things. This doesn't mean the end of the sorrow, anxiety, and bitterness of suffering. However, the crosses are no longer crosses but God. In the former stages, the cross was virtue, and it was more and more exalted as the condition advanced. Here, the soul experiences the cross to be God, like everything else. All that constitutes the life of this soul, all that it has, moment by moment, is God to it.

The outward appearance of these people is quite ordinary, with nothing unusual to be observed in them except by those who are able

Spiritual Rivers

to understand them. Everything is seen in God, and in its true light. Therefore, this condition is not subject to deception. There are no visions, revelations, ecstasies, raptures, or transformations. None of these things belong to this state because it is above them all. This way is simple, pure, and naked. It sees everything as God sees it, with his eyes.

Ten

The Resurrection Life

This is where true freedom begins. It's not a freedom, as some imagine, that requires idleness. That would be imprisonment rather than freedom, imagining ourselves free because, having an aversion to our own works, we no longer practice them. This freedom is different. It easily does all things that God wills to be done, and the longer and more painfully we were unable to do them before, the more easily we can do them now.

I confess that I don't understand the resurrection state of Christians who, professing that they have attained it, remain powerless and destitute throughout their lives. The works of

Spiritual Rivers

resurrected people are the works of life. If the soul remains lifeless, I say that while it may be dead or buried, it is not risen. A risen soul should be able to perform—without difficulty—all the works that it has performed in the past, but now they will be done in God. Didn't Lazarus, after his resurrection, perform all the duties of life as before? Wasn't Jesus Christ, after his resurrection, willing to eat and talk with others? Those who believe themselves to be risen with Christ but are nevertheless stunted in their spiritual growth and incapable of devotion—I say that they do not possess a resurrection life because in that state, everything is restored to the soul a hundredfold.

There is a beautiful illustration of this in the case of Job, whose story I consider to be a mirror of the spiritual life. First God robbed him of his wealth, which we may think of as gifts and graces. Then he takes his children. This represents the destruction of natural emotions and our own works, which are like our children, our most cherished possessions. Then God deprived Job of

The Resurrection Life

his health, which symbolizes the loss of virtue. Then he touched his person, making him an object of horror and contempt. It even appears that this holy man was guilty of sin, failing in his despair. His friends accused him of being justly punished for his crimes. There was no healthy part left in him. But after he had been brought down to the dung hill, reduced as it were to a corpse, God restored everything to him—his wealth, his children, his health, and his life.

It's the same with spiritual resurrection. Everything is restored but with a wonderful power to use it without being defiled by it, grasping it but without appropriating it as before. Everything is done in God. It's here that we find true freedom and true life. As Paul writes, "If we have been united with him in a death like his, we will certainly also be united with him in a resurrection like his." Can there be true freedom where there are powerlessness and limitations? No. "If the son makes you free, you will be free indeed"—but with *his* freedom.

Spiritual Rivers

This then is where true liberty begins. Nothing that God desires is difficult for us or costs us anything. If we are called to preach, to teach, and so on, we do it with amazing ability and without the need to prepare our lessons. We're able to work just as Jesus commanded his disciples: "Don't worry about how you will defend yourselves. For I will give you words and wisdom that none of your adversaries will be able to resist or contradict." This isn't given until after we've experienced powerlessness, and the deeper that experience has been, the greater is the freedom.

It's useless to try to force ourselves into this condition. Because God would not be the source, we would not obtain the desired results. Within this resurrected life, all good things are given. The soul can't practice virtues as virtues—it's not even conscious of them—but the virtues have become so habitual to that soul that it practices them naturally, almost instinctively. When it hears others talk of deep humiliation, the soul's

The Resurrection Life

surprised to find that it experiences nothing of the kind. In order to be humbled, we must be something, but nothingness cannot be lowered. The soul's present condition is also higher than all humility and all virtue though its transformation into God. Thus its powerlessness arises both from its annihilation and its elevation.

These people have nothing to outwardly distinguish them from others, unless it is that they do no harm to anyone. They are quite ordinary, so they do not attract attention. They live in a state of quiet rest, free from all care and anxiety. They experience a deep joy that comes from the absence of fear, desire, or longing. Nothing can disturb their rest or diminish their joy. David possessed this experience when he said, "The Lord is my light and my salvation — whom shall I fear? The Lord is the stronghold of my life — of whom shall I be afraid?"

Poverty-stricken, weary ones, how well you are repaid. What a gain you made in exchange for all your losses. Could you have believed, when

Spiritual Rivers

you were lying in the dust, that what caused you so much horror could have procured for you the great happiness you now possess? If someone had told you, you would not have believed it. Learn now through your own experience how good it is to trust in God and that those who put their confidence in him will never be defeated.

How much weariness might the soul have been rescued from if it had known how to let God work. But we are not willing to abandon ourselves and trust only in God. Even those who appear to do so, who think themselves well established in it, are only abandoned in imagination, not in reality. They are willing to abandon themselves in one thing but not in another. They want to compromise with God, to place a limit to what they will permit him to do. They want to give themselves up but only on this or that condition. That isn't abandonment. An entire and total abandonment excludes nothing, holds back nothing—neither death, nor life, nor progress, nor holiness, nor heaven, nor hell.

Eleven

The Abandoned Soul

Having attained a divine state, the soul is an immovable rock, resistant to all blows or shocks unless the Lord desires it to do something uncustomary. In that case, if the soul fails to yield to his first promptings, it suffers the pain of a constraint to which it can offer no resistance and is compelled by a violence that cannot be explained to obey God's will.

It's impossible to explain the strange tests to which God subjects the hearts that are perfectly abandoned and offer no resistance to him in anything. If I could talk about them, I would not be understood. All I can say is that he doesn't leave them even the shadow of anything

Spiritual Rivers

that can be named, either within God or apart from God. He raises them above everything through the loss of everything so that on earth or in heaven, nothing less than God himself can stop them. Nothing can harm them because nothing is hurtful for them anymore because of their union with God. That union contracts no defilement in associating with sinners because of its essential purity.

This is more real than I can express. The soul participates in the purity of God. Because all natural purity has been annihilated, the purity of God exists in the soul's nothingness—and so truly that the heart is perfectly ignorant of evil, powerless to commit it. This does not prevent the possibility of the soul falling away, but the profound nothingness of the soul doesn't leave anything that can be appropriated to itself, and appropriation alone causes sin. That which no longer exists cannot sin.

The peace of those in this state is so constant and so profound that nothing in earth or hell

The Abandoned Soul

can disturb it even for a moment. The physical senses are still susceptible to suffering, but when these people are overpowered by suffering and cry out with anguish, if they are questioned or examine themselves, they find nothing within themselves that suffers. In the midst of the greatest pain, they say that they suffer nothing. They're unable to admit that they are suffering because of the divine state of blessedness that reigns in the center or supreme part of themselves. There is such an entire and complete separation of these two parts, the inferior and the superior, that they live together like strangers. The most extraordinary trouble does not interrupt the perfect peace, tranquility, joy, and rest of the superior part, while the joy of the divine life does not prevent the suffering of the inferior.

If you wish to attribute any goodness to those who are thus transformed in God, they will object to it because they cannot find anything in themselves that can be named, affirmed, or heard. They are in a complete negation. This is why writers have so many different terms and expressions about this subject. They find it difficult to make themselves understood except by those whose experience matches with their own.

Another effect of this negation is that the soul, having lost all that was its own because God has substituted himself, can attribute nothing either to itself or to God. It knows God alone, and about him, it can say nothing. In this place, everything is God to the soul. It's no longer a matter of seeing all things in God because seeing things in God means distinguishing those things from him. If I were to enter a room, for example, I would see everything that is in the room in addition to the room itself. But if everything were removed from the room, then I would only see the room.

In this negation, all creatures—heavenly, earthly, or spiritual—disappear and fade away, and only God himself remains. The soul only sees God everywhere. Everything is God, not through thought, sight, or enlightenment but

The Abandoned Soul

through the identity of this state, through the consummation of union. This makes the soul see God through participation in God so that it cannot see itself. It can't see *any* created thing apart from the uncreated God. The only uncreated one is everything and is in everything.

People might condemn such a state, saying it makes us something less than the lowliest insect—and so it does, not through obstinacy and resolution but through powerlessness to interfere with ourselves.

You might ask someone in this state, "Who made you do this or that thing? Did God tell you to do it? Has he revealed his will about this to you?"

"I have no idea," the person will say. "I don't even think about understanding anything. Everything is God and his will. I no longer understand what you mean by 'the will of God' because his will has become a part of me."

"But why do you do this thing rather than that thing?"

Spiritual Rivers

"I don't know. I merely let myself by guided by the one who guides me."

"But *why*?"

"Because I'm carried along with God. I'm guided by him alone. He goes here or there. He is the one who acts, and I am merely a tool in his hands that I neither see nor care about. He guides me because I'm no longer anything. I have no separate interest because through the loss of myself I have lost all self-interest. I can't give any reasons for my actions because I don't have any actions of my own. However, I act infallibly so long as I have no other nature than that of the infallible God."

This kind of blind abandonment is the permanent condition of the soul about which I speak. Having become one with God, it can see nothing but God. Having lost all separateness, self-possession, and distinction, it can no longer abandon itself. The soul in this state is "hidden with Christ in God," mingled with him like the river that we've discussed is mingled with

The Abandoned Soul

the sea so that it can no longer be separate. It has the ebb and flow of the sea—no longer by choice, desire, and freedom but by nature. The immense sea has absorbed the river's shallow, limited waters so that they now participate in all the movements of the sea. The sea carries it, but it's not even carried because it has lost its own being and has no motion except the motion of the sea. It acts as the sea acts, not because it has the same qualities as the sea but because, having lost all its own, natural qualities, it has no other qualities but those of the sea. It has no power to ever be anything but sea. It's not that the river could not in a moment be separate from the sea. If God chose, he could remove the soul from his arms, but he doesn't do this, so the earthly creature acts as if it were divine.

Some might say that I deprive humans of their freedom with this idea. Not so. They are no longer free only through an excess of freedom, having freely lost all created freedom and to take their place in uncreated freedom, which is not reduced,

Spiritual Rivers

restricted, or limited by anything. The soul's freedom is so great, so broad, that the whole earth seems like a speck of dust to which the soul is not confined. It's free to do everything and nothing. It can accommodate itself to any status or condition. It can do all things, but it takes no part in them. Glorious state, who can describe you? What do you have to fear or worry about?

Paul could say, "Who will separate us from the love of Christ? I am convinced that neither death nor life, neither angels nor demons, neither the present nor the future nor any powers, neither height nor depth nor anything else in all creation, will be able to separate us from the love of God that is in Christ Jesus our Lord." These words, "I am convinced," exclude all doubt. So what was the foundation of Paul's confidence? It was in the infallibility of God alone. The letters of this great apostle, this mystical teacher, are often read but seldom understood. Paul describes the entire mystic path — its beginning, its progress, its conclusion — and even the divine

The Abandoned Soul

life. Few are able to understand it, but those who are given the understanding see it all as clear as day in Paul's letters.

If those who find it so difficult to give themselves to God could only experience this state, they would profess that although the path is arduous, a single day of this life is sufficient payment for years of trouble. But God brings the soul here by ways altogether opposed to human wisdom and imagination. He builds up by tearing down. He gives life by killing. If I could only explain what he does, the strange methods he uses to bring us here. There is no need for place or time here. Everything is the same. All places are good, and wherever God's plans take us, it is well because all means are useless and infinitely surpassed when we have reached the end. There is nothing left to wish for. But silence! People are not able to hear it. Those who have experienced it know what it is.

Everything is God in this place. God is everywhere and in everything, so everything is the same to the soul. Its religion is God himself—always the same, never interrupted. If sometimes God pours some stream of his glory upon the soul's natural strengths and emotions, it has no effect upon the core because the core is always the same. The soul is indifferent to solitude or a crowd. It no longer looks forward to leaving the body in order to be united with God. It is now not only united with God but transformed, changed into the object of its love, so that it no longer thinks of loving. It loves God with his own love—naturally, though not irrevocably.

Twelve

Deformity

An analogy comes to mind—the analogy of grain—that seems quite fitting for this subject. First, the grain is separated from the husk. This illustrates conversion and separation from sin. When the grain is separated from the husk and pure, it must be ground by affliction, burdens, sickness, and so on. When it is thus bruised and reduced to flour, there is nothing impure to remove because that has been taken away, but coarseness, the bran, must still be removed. When there is nothing left refined flour, it can be made into bread to feed others. Now it seems as if the flour is soiled, darkened, and blighted—that its refinement and whiteness are

Spiritual Rivers

taken from it in order to make the dough that is far less beautiful than the flour. Finally, this dough is exposed to the heat of the oven. This is exactly what happens to the soul I have been talking about. But after the bread is baked, it is fit for the mouth of the king. He not unites it with himself by eating it, consuming it, digesting it—annihilating it—so that it can enter his body and become part of himself.

You will notice that although the king has eaten the bread, which is the greatest honor that the bread can receive and which is its end, it cannot have union with the substance of the king unless it is annihilated by digestion, losing all its natural form and characteristics. This state of union is quite different from the state of transformation. In order to become one with God, to be changed into him, the soul must not only be eaten but digested. Only after having lost everything that was its own can the soul become one with God himself: "May they all be one, Father, just as you are in me and I am in you. May they

Deformity

be one as we are one—I in them and you in me—so that they may be brought to complete unity." Also: "Whoever is united with the Lord is one with him in spirit."

These people appear quite ordinary, as I have said, because they have nothing outward that distinguishes them—except for unlimited freedom. This freedom often scandalizes those who are limited and confined within themselves because they can see nothing better than what they have themselves. Everything that's different from what they have seems to be evil. However, the holiness of these simple and innocent ones whom they despise is a holiness incomparably higher than everything that they think of as holy. Their own works, though performed with such strictness, have no more strength than the source from which they are performed, and although it is lifted up and ennobled, this source is always the effort of a weak creature.

Those who are fulfilled with this divine union act in God have a source of infinite strength, so

Spiritual Rivers

even their smallest actions are more pleasing to God than the multitude of heroic deeds achieved by others that appear so great in the sight of people. The ones in this stage of spiritual life don't look for great things to do but rest in the contentment of being what God makes them at each moment. Without doing anything, they do more to convert a kingdom than five hundred preachers who have not attained this condition. If people only understood the glory that is given to God by these whom the world scorns, they would be astonished. These give to God a glory that is worthy of himself because God, acting within them, brings into them a glory worthy of himself. God hides them in his arms, under the cover of a most ordinary life, so that they may be known to him alone.

Here the secrets of God are revealed in himself and in the hearts of those in whom he dwells. They are not revealed through word, sight, or insight but through the understanding of God that abides in God. When these people

Deformity

have to write or speak, they themselves are astonished to find that everything flows forth from a divine source, without their having been aware that they possessed such treasures. They find themselves in the midst of a profound understanding, like a priceless treasure that isn't seen until it needs to be revealed. By showing it to others, it's revealed to them as well. It's not so with other Christians, whose insight comes from their own experience. For people in this state, the soul itself no longer exists, no longer acts, but God acts and uses the soul as his instrument. God includes all treasures within himself and shows them to others through the soul. Thus, as the soul draws these treasures from its center, it becomes aware of their presence even though it has never reflected upon them before.

Those of the first stage see things and enjoy them as we enjoy the sun, but these people have become one with the sun itself, which does not enjoy or reflect upon its own light. This latter condition is permanent. Its only change, so far as

Spiritual Rivers

its center is concerned, is a greater advancement in God. Because God is infinite, he can continually make the soul more divine by enlarging its capacity, just as the river that we have discussed expands in proportion as it is lost in the sea, continually merging with the sea without ever leaving it. So it is for these souls.

Everyone in this stage has God, but they each have him more or less fully. They are all filled with him, but they do not all have the same abundance. A small vase, when full, is truly just as filled as a large vase, but it does not contain an equal amount of water. In the same way, all of these souls are filled with the fullness of God, but they are filled according to their capacity, and it is this capacity that God continually enlarges. Therefore, the longer Christians live in this divine condition, the more they expand.

Their capacity continually grows, but they have nothing more to do or desire because they always have God in his fullness, and he never leaves an empty corner in their hearts. As they

Deformity

grow and enlarge, he fills them with himself. We see this with air. A small room is full of air, but a large room contains more. If you continually increase the size of a room, to the same degree air will increase, imperceptibly but without fail. In the same way, without changing its condition or disposition, and without any new awareness, the soul increases in capacity and abundance. However, this growing capacity can only be received in a state of nothingness. In any other condition, there is opposition to growth.

It might be good to explain what appears to be a contradiction. I say that the soul must be reduced to nothing in order to enter into God and that it must lose everything that is its own, yet I speak about the capacity that the soul retains. There are two types of capacity. One type of capacity is natural to the creature, and this is narrow and limited. When it's purified, the creature is able to receive the gifts of God but not God himself. Anything that we receive within ourselves must necessarily be smaller than

Spiritual Rivers

ourselves, just as anything enclosed within a vase must be smaller than the vase—even if it's more valuable than the vase.

The second type of capacity is a capacity to expand and lose itself more and more in God. It comes after the soul has lost stopped appropriating things to itself, which confined it to itself. This capacity is no longer limited because the soul's annihilation has removed its form, allowing the soul to flow into God. It loses itself and flows into him who is beyond comprehension. The more the soul is lost in him, the more it expands and becomes immense, participating in his perfections and being more and more transformed in him, just as the river that flows into its source, the sea, continually merges with it. God, who is our source, has created us with a nature that is ready to be united, transformed, and made one with him.

Thirteen

Union with God

The soul that is united with God has nothing to do now but remain as it is, following all the direction of its guide without resistance. All its motions are from God, and he guides it perfectly. It wasn't like this with the previous conditions—except in those moments when the soul began to taste the center. It was not so infallible then, however, so those who apply this principle to any but the most advanced state would be deceived.

For this soul, its duty now is to blindly follow all the directions of God. All reflection is banished here, and the soul would find it difficult to indulge in reflection, even if it wanted to. The

Spiritual Rivers

soul might with some effort accomplish reflection, but this should be carefully avoided because reflection alone has the power of leading people to enter back into themselves and thus draw away from God. Those who do not go out from God will not sin. If they do sin, then, it's because they have gone out from God. This can only be caused by self-appropriation. The soul can only take itself back from its abandonment through reflective action, and this would become a hell for the soul, just like that of the great angel who, by looking at himself with self-satisfaction and preferring himself to God, became a devil. Such a condition would be just as terrible for the soul as the condition that it had reached had been advanced.

Some might argue that suffering is impossible in this condition, not only in the center but also in the senses, because there must be natural reactions in order for there to be suffering and because reflection constitutes the principal and the most painful part of suffering. All this is true in a certain sense, but just as it is true that less

Union with God

advanced souls sometimes suffer through reflection and sometimes through experience, I maintain that it is also true that souls in this condition cannot suffer except through experience. This does not imply that the sorrow will be limited and less intense than the sorrow of reflection. The burns of one brought into actual contact with fire will much more severe than those of one burned by the reflection of fire.

It might be said that God can teach them through reflection how to suffer. However, God will not use reflection for this purpose. He can show them in an instant how to suffer with a direct, not reflected, view of suffering, just as those in heaven see in God all that is within God. They see all that flows out from God to his creatures without looking at these things or reflecting upon them. They remain fully absorbed and lost in God.

This is what deceives so many spiritually minded people. They imagine that nothing can be known or suffered except through reflection.

Spiritual Rivers

On the contrary, that kind of knowledge and suffering is slight in comparison to the knowledge and suffering that is given in other ways. All the suffering that can be defined and understood, even when expressed in exaggerated terms, doesn't equal the suffering of those who do not know they suffer, who cannot even admit that they suffer because of the great separation between experience and reflection. It is true that they suffer extreme pain, but it is also true that they suffer nothing and remain in a state of perfect contentment. I believe that if such a soul were taken to hell, it would suffer all the cruel tortures of its fate in a complete contentment because of the supreme happiness of its transformed center. This is the cause of the indifference that they feel towards all conditions. As I have said, this contentment does not prevent them from experiencing the extremity of suffering, but the extremity of suffering does not hinder their perfect happiness. Those who have experienced it will understand me.

Union with God

This state is not like the passive state of love. In that state, the soul is filled with a love of suffering and of the good pleasure of God. In this state, the will is lost through the soul's union with God. Everything is God without its being recognized as such. The soul is founded upon this condition of sovereign, unchangeable goodness. It rests in a perfect blessedness. Nothing can mar the soul's perfect happiness, and this becomes its permanent condition. Many possess or experience this happiness temporarily before it becomes their permanent condition. God first gives the knowledge of the condition. Then he gives a desire for it. Then he gives it obscurely and indistinctly. Last, he makes it a normal condition and establishes the soul in that condition forever.

It might be said that when once the soul is established in this condition, nothing more can be done for it. It's just the opposite. There are infinite things to be done on the part of God but none on the part of the creature. God does

Spiritual Rivers

not create the divine life all at once but only in stages. Then, as I have said, he enlarges the capacity of the soul, making it more and more godly, because the magnitude of God cannot be measured.

Oh Lord, "how abundant is your goodness, which you have stored up for those who fear you!" It was the sight of this state of blessedness that drew such frequent exclamations from David after he had been purified from sin. These people cannot be troubled by sin. Although they hate it infinitely, they no longer suffer from it. They see it as God sees it. If it were necessary and if God willed it, they would give their lives to prevent the commission of a single sin. However, they are without action, without desire, without inclination, without choice, without impatience. They are in a state of complete death, seeing things only as God sees them and judging them only with God's judgment.

www.ingramcontent.com/pod-product-compliance
Lightning Source LLC
Chambersburg PA
CBHW051343040426
42453CB00007B/389